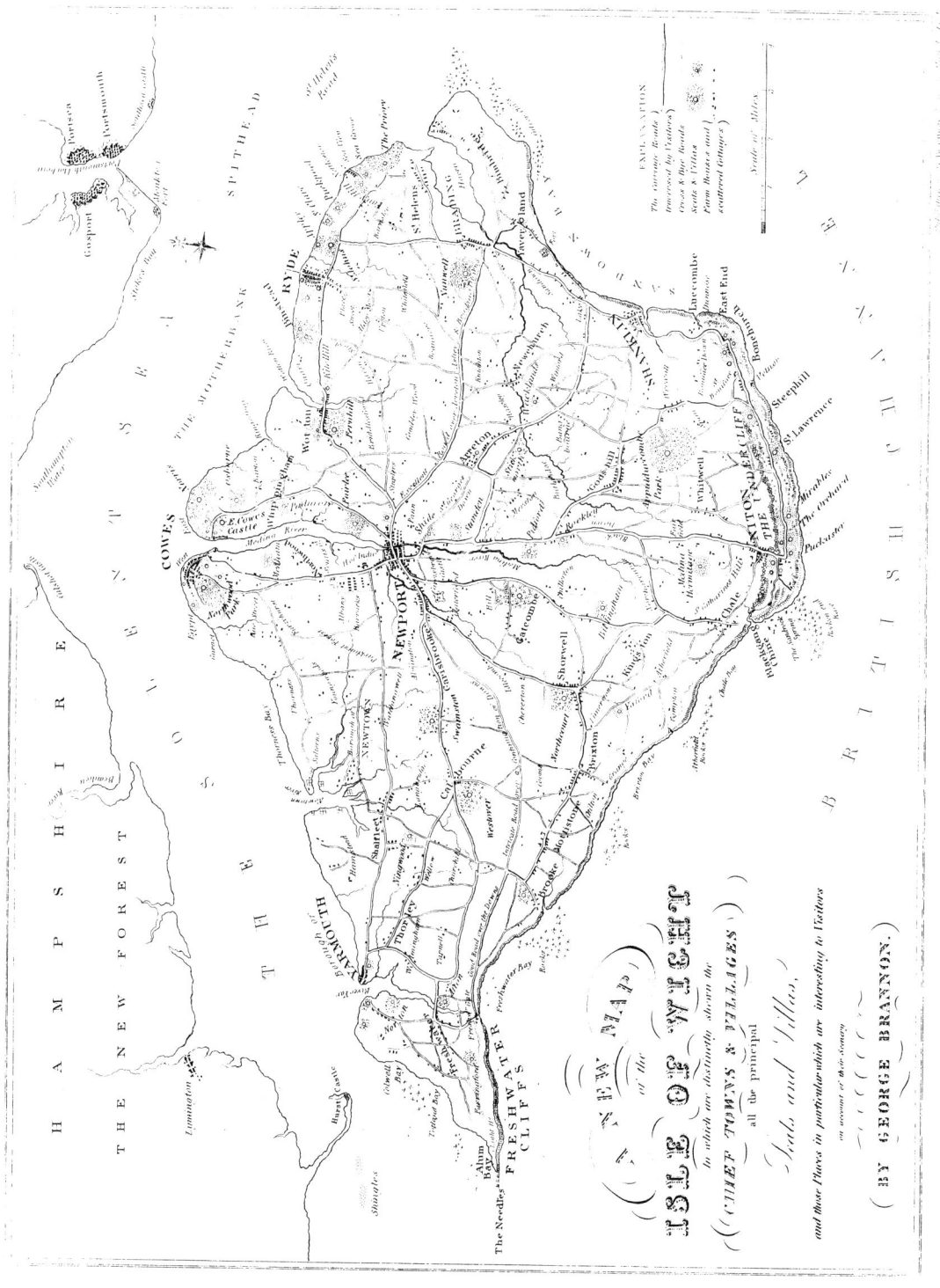

HISTORIC PARKS AND GARDENS

OF THE

ISLE OF WIGHT

VICKY BASFORD

Assisted by:

Frank Basford
Roy Brinton
David Motkin

ISLE OF WIGHT COUNTY COUNCIL
CULTURAL SERVICES DEPARTMENT
1989

FIRST PUBLISHED:	1989
	© ISLE OF WIGHT COUNTY COUNCIL, 1989
I.S.B.N.	0-906328-42-X
PRINTED BY:	WEST ISLAND PRINTERS LIMITED, AFTON ROAD, FRESHWATER, ISLE OF WIGHT, PO40 9TT Tel: (0983) 753161/754683
PUBLISHED BY:	ISLE OF WIGHT COUNTY COUNCIL, CULTURAL SERVICES DEPARTMENT, HEADQUARTERS, PARKHURST ROAD, NEWPORT, ISLE OF WIGHT PO30 5TX

FRONT COVER
Appuldurcombe Park. Engraving by George Brannon.

BACK COVER
Ornamental Stone Lion, Woodlands Vale (Photo. Frank Basford).

CONTENTS

FOREWORD	7
ACKNOWLEDGEMENTS	8
PREFACE	9
INTRODUCTION	11
MEDIEVAL DEER PARKS	13
EARLY GARDENS	18
LATER PARKS AND GARDENS	29
PARKS AND GARDENS TODAY AND IN THE FUTURE	61
GAZETTEER	65
PARKS AND GARDENS OPEN TO THE PUBLIC	71
REFERENCES	72
INDEX	78

ILLUSTRATIONS

Colour Plates

Newtown from the air, showing garden plots	33
Woolverton Manor, Shorwell	33
Blaeu's map of the Isle of Wight, 1645	33
Map of Appuldurcombe Park, c.1800	34
Appuldurcombe Inner Park and Ha-ha	34
'The Temple', Swainston, 1987	34
Westover Park from the Ornamental Lake	34
Fernhill, from Wootton Creek	39
Norris Castle Ornamental Farm	39
Osborne, Italianate Terraces	39
Nunwell, Formal Garden	39
Barton Manor Garden	40
Urn within Oriental Garden, Woodlands Vale	40
The Temperate House, Ventnor Botanic Gardens	40
Vernon Square, Ryde	40

Illustrations in Text

Frontispiece: Isle of Wight Map, G. Brannon 1824	2
Isle of Wight Deer Parks	15
'Waching Park', from Speed's 1611 Map	15
Reconstruction of Brading Roman Villa	18
Lea's Map of Newport, 1689	21
Plan of Carisbrooke Castle in the time of Edward I	21
Appuldurcombe Tudor House and Garden	24
Knighton Gorges House and Walled Garden	24
Engraving of Northcourt House and Gardens, 1796	27
Map of Nunwell, 1748	27
Ordnance Survey of Swainston and North Park, 1791	31
Appuldurcombe Estate Map of 1773	37
Plan of Appuldurcombe, showing expansion of Park	38
Cooke's Castle, St. Martin's Down	43
Freemantle Gate, Appuldurcombe Park	43
Engraving of Appuldurcombe Park	44
Detail from engraving of Nunwell Park	44
Engraving of 'Old' Osborne House and Park	46
Engraving of Gatcombe Park	47
Engraving of Sea Cottage, St. Lawrence	51
Lodge, Northwood Park	53
The Marina, St. John's	55
Engraving of East Cowes Castle	55
Design for East Cowes Botanical Gardens	59
'The Temple', Swainston, 1985	63

FOREWORD

This book describes for the first time the valuable heritage of historic parks and gardens possessed by the Isle of Wight, a heritage that has perhaps been undervalued in the past. Some parks and gardens mentioned in the text no longer survive, but those which do should be appreciated as important features of our Island landscape, to be conserved for the enjoyment of present and future generations of Islanders and visitors.

The study of historic parks and gardens forms part of a wider Countryside Heritage Study of the Island which was initiated by the Amenities and Countryside Committee of the Isle of Wight County Council in 1983. An introductory booklet proposing topics for study was published in 1984 and research on old grasslands and ancient woodland was subsequently carried out. Parks and Gardens forms the third topic of the Countryside Heritage Study project. Further studies will be necessary to provide additional information regarding the Island's Countryside, notably on other aspects of the man-made landscape, and on rivers, wetlands and coastlands.

No conservation is possible without adequate knowledge. The County Archaeological Unit's Sites and Monuments and Historic Buildings Records provide essential databases of information on the Island's man-made monuments and landscape, to which information collected during the Parks and Gardens study will be added.

Positive help for the Island's countryside heritage, including advice on grants, conservation work and tree-planting schemes, can be offered by the Island Planning Unit, the County Archaeological Unit, and the Countryside Management Service. Much valuable work is also carried out by groups such as the local branch of the British Trust for Conservation Volunteers, the Isle of Wight Natural History and Archaeological Society and the Isle of Wight Society.

This year marks the establishment of The Isle of Wight Gardens Trust. The principal aims of the Trust are to protect, conserve and enhance parks and gardens and to encourage greater knowledge and enjoyment of them throughout the Island.

Chairman, IWCC Amenities and Countryside Committee
March 1989

ACKNOWLEDGEMENTS

The present publication arises from a survey undertaken for the Amenities and Countryside Committee of the Isle of Wight County Council. I should like to thank members of this committee for their support and encouragement. The Isle of Wight Buildings Preservation Trust gave a grant towards the initial survey and has now generously funded the further work needed to compile this book, which is a joint production by the Isle of Wight County Council Cultural Services Department and the Island Planning Unit.

During the preparation of the book, I have been particularly grateful for help and advice from Geoff Cadman, Assistant Island Planning Officer, and Dr. David Tomalin, County Archaeological Officer. The County Archivist, Clifford Webster, has kindly drawn my attention to archival material which might otherwise have been overlooked. Assistance in documentary research has been provided by Philip Ratcliffe and Stuart Traves of the Island Planning Unit. The manuscript was typed by Elaine Affleck.

I am especially indebted to Clive Chatters for access to his unpublished research notes on Watchingwell Park and Parkhurst Forest, to Dr. Colin Pope for information on tree lichens in medieval parkland and to Mark Tosdevin for material regarding Brading Roman Villa.

Many others, including John Harrison, Johanna Jones, Gwen Lacey, Jim O'Donnell, Malcolm Pinhorn, Bill Shepard and Ian Smith have supplied information or advised on the text. I am grateful to all the garden owners who have supplied information or granted access to their grounds.

The cover was designed by Roger Flynn, Graphic Designer, County Architect's Department. The colour plates are the work of: 1 and 2 – David Tomalin; 4 and 5 – Ben Houfton; 6, 7, 9, and 13 – - Frank Basford; 11 – Vicky Basford; 14 – Simon Goodenough; 15 – - Ian Smith. The black and white photograph of the Swainston temple was taken by Marion Brinton and further photographic work was carried out by Joe Paterson. I am grateful to Mr. A.M. Goddard of Barton Manor for permission to reproduce Plate 12; to the Trustees of Carisbrooke Castle Museum for illustrations of Knighton, Northcourt and the Marina, St. John's; to Mrs. Maud Hoyle for the photograph of Northwood Park Lodge; and to Mrs Oglander for permission to reproduce the Nunwell map. Caroline Ball, Andrew Wyld and Colonel and Mrs. Aylmer have kindly permitted me to include photographs of their properties.

My husband, Frank Basford, has carried out much field work relating to the study of Parks and Gardens on the Isle of Wight, and this book could not have been completed without his help and encouragement.

Vicky Basford
March 1989

PREFACE

Historic parks and gardens, both nationally and locally, are of value for many reasons (Banks *et al* 1983, 59–65). The history of parks and gardens is closely linked to the history of art and to the history of ideas, particularly in the most creative period of English garden development – the eighteenth century. Appreciation of landscape as a whole and of British as well as foreign landscape is intimately connected with the development of landscape parks.

A well planned design is perhaps the major factor in the creation of visually attractive parkland. Within the confines of a garden however, the choice, colour and arrangement of flowers and shrubs provide a major contribution to its beauty. A large part of the history of parks and gardens is concerned with the development of plants and with the increasing availability of different species of flowering plants and shrubs since the sixteenth century. Development of this botanic theme is regretfully beyond the scope of this book but further research into the planting history of individual gardens and a study of extant trees and shrubs within these gardens would be of great value.

The historical value of parks and gardens lies in the fact that each site constitutes a unique record, providing evidence of the way in which changes in fashion have influenced the development of the particular garden or designed landscape. The value of a particular site is dependant upon the extent to which documentary evidence survives, and its relationship with the evidence on the ground. A further factor influencing value is the extent to which the site is representative of the work of a particular designer or of a recognised style or fashion.

Parks and gardens can tell us much about the social relationships of times past (Williamson and Bellamy 1987). Medieval deer parks and eighteenth and nineteenth century landscape parks may be considered as status symbols revealing the importance of conspicuous display. The process of emparkment on the Isle of Wight mirrors to some extent the same process on the mainland. The enlargement of parks such as those at Gatcombe and Appuldurcombe in the second half of the eighteenth century would appear to have taken place with little regard for the rights of the local villagers, whose fields and sometimes even cottages seem to have been destroyed in the interests of the grand plan.

The incorporation of earlier landscape features within parks gives them a considerable archaeological value which until recently has not been fully recognised. The remains of early field systems, ancient trees and abandoned houses amounting sometimes to complete medieval landscapes are often incorporated within eighteenth century parklands. Early gardens themselves are occasionally preserved as earthworks, an aspect of our archaeological heritage which had been almost completely overlooked until recent years (Taylor 1983). The incorporation of ancient trees, woodland, hedges and grassland within landscape parks makes them also of great importance to the ecologist.

PREFACE

The designers of landscape parks utilised not only natural components such as grassland, trees and water, but also architectural features such as The Temple at Swainston, Cook's Castle at Appuldurcombe and the lodges at St. John's, Ryde. These features played an extremely important part in the overall design concept. Many of them have now vanished, but others survive including lodges and estate cottages at Northwood Park and Westover Park, a 'gothic' folly at St. John's, Ryde, and the Freemantle Gate at Appuldurcombe. These are usually, but not always, legally protected as listed buildings. Individual surviving features such as garden walls, follies, ice houses and trees clearly have heritage value and merit conservation as do complete parks and gardens, where these survive.

INTRODUCTION

Despite its popular title of the "Garden Isle", the historic gardens and designed landscapes of the Isle of Wight have received little attention in recent years. Perhaps this is because there are so many picturesque landscapes on the Island which seem to have been designed by nature rather than by art: the dramatic white cliffs of The Needles headland, the romantic backdrop of the Undercliff, the natural gardens formed by the Chines and the panoramic views from the tops of the Downs. It was precisely this picturesque quality of landscape that attracted early tourists to the Island. These late eighteenth century travellers were the first to appreciate fully the beauties of British, rather than foreign, scenery, particularly if the scenery was sufficiently dramatic or romantic. Designed landscapes such as Appuldurcombe Park were definitely on the itinerary of these discriminating visitors. Those who chose to settle on the Island preferred the romantic coastal landscapes in which to construct their marine villas and cottages ornées which were set in attractive grounds. Pre-eminent among the coastal residences of the nineteenth century was Osborne, purchased by Queen Victoria and Prince Albert as their holiday retreat. Osborne was indeed planned to fit a landscape. Albert compared the Solent in summer to the Bay of Naples and so an Italianate style was chosen for the house and garden.

It was the whole Island landscape, rather than individual grounds, which prompted the epithet of "Garden Isle". Nevertheless we should not underestimate the contribution of these pleasure grounds to the flowering of the Garden Isle. Even today there is a diversity of settings for historic Island houses both great and small that seems to fit their character to perfection: the faded grandeur of Appuldurcombe with the shell of the stately house standing in a well-designed inner park, while beyond are the sad remains of a vast designed landscape; Gatcombe House framed against woodland which also shelters the tiny church; Westover set in serene parkland mirrored in the miniature lake; and Mottistone where the modern garden set in a sheltered combe superbly complements the Tudor manor house.

To trace the history of the Island's parks and gardens we must go back in time beyond the era of those discriminating tourists who first 'discovered' the Isle of Wight. The ornamental landscape parks of the eighteenth century were in some ways the cultural successors to the deer parks of the Middle Ages which themselves could be ornamental as well as functional and which sometimes evolved directly into landscape parks. The inspiration for garden design in Britain came ultimately from the classical world although it was not until the Renaissance that the true potential of the garden as an art form was realised in Britain. On the Isle of Wight very few remains of parks or gardens earlier than the eighteenth century survive, although we can piece together the history of these early parks and pleasure grounds from the study of old maps and documents. Designed landscapes and gardens from the eighteenth century and onwards do exist although often only the skeleton of the design survives.

INTRODUCTION

This book attempts to set out what is known of the Island's historic parks and gardens. It is based on a survey carried out for the Island Planning Unit (Basford 1987). The survey examined printed sources, maps and air photographs. Manuscript sources were also studied for a limited number of sites. It was not possible to carry out systematic fieldwork within the time available. The book should therefore be considered as a stimulus for further research rather than as a definitive statement.

It must be emphasised that many of the parks and gardens described in this book are private property and may **not** be open to the public. A list of those places currently open to the public is given at the end of the book.

MEDIEVAL DEER PARKS

Deer parks were essentially a creation of the Normans who introduced the fallow deer into England, probably in the twelfth century (Rackham 1986, 49). Fallow deer were easier to manage within enclosed parks than either red or roe deer. Parks did, however, exist before the twelfth century. There is one reference to a mainland deer park which predates the Norman Conquest and thirty-five are recorded throughout England in the Domesday Book (Rackham 1986, 123). By the thirteenth century there were many parks; from then on anybody wishing to empark land had to obtain a licence from the king.

During medieval times deer were preserved both within forests and within deer parks. A forest was a relatively large area of land to which special forest laws applied, restricting the rights of the inhabitants in the interest of preserving the deer and its habitat. Each forest contained a nucleus of unenclosed land which might be woodland, moorland, heath or fen, but part of the area covered by forest law might include settlements, farmland and open pasture. The deer within the forest were owned by the king or by a great landowner. A deer park was a relatively small area of land, averaging about 200 acres, which was enclosed by a bank and a ditch. The bank was surmounted by a deer-proof fence called a 'park pale'. Deer parks were owned by great lords and magnates of the church and by the Crown; later they were also owned by lesser gentry and religious houses.

Most deer parks contained both trees and grassland. This characteristic combination of grassland and scattered trees is known as 'wood pasture' and is a recognisable component of the English landscape which occurs also on common land and in medieval forests.

Medieval deer parks have been commonly regarded as hunting preserves but this was not their primary function (Rackham 1986, 125). They could be the scene of hunts but were generally too small to offer much scope for a good chase. The real function of deer parks and indeed of the royal forests was the supply of venison, an especially valued meat, at a time when fresh meat was hard to obtain during the winter months. Nevertheless, despite their predominantly practical function, deer parks were very expensive to create and to maintain and their value as medieval status symbols should not be overlooked.

The history of deer parks on the Isle of Wight predates 1086, for the Domesday Book records the creation of "The King's Park" at Watchingwell, which involved taking half a hide of land from the adjoining manor of Watchingwell owned by the nuns of Wilton Abbey. The Domesday Book reference makes Watchingwell one of the oldest known deer parks in England. It was 350 acres in size (Page ed. 1912, 227) and was situated on the south-west corner of Parkhurst Forest, or Avington Forest as it was sometimes called, from which it was separated by the track later known as "Betty Haunt Lane". Parkhurst itself was probably not technically a forest in the early Middle Ages but was the hunting ground, or chase, of the lords of the Island. From the end of the fourteenth century, however, it remained with the Crown and is entered as "The King's Forest" on some maps as late as 1791. The nearby "King's Park" of Watchingwell may also have passed from royal control when the Island was granted to the de Redvers family in about 1100, coming back under royal control when the Crown regained the Island in 1293.

It is likely that the functions of Watchingwell Park and Parkhurst were interconnected, Watchingwell being used for the breeding of deer which were then released into the forest. A parallel for this juxtaposition of park and forest exists at Gillingham in Dorset (Cantor and Wilson 1961, 110). In the fourteenth century there are references to "Old Park" and "New Park" at Watchingwell (Kökeritz 1940, 104). The reference to "New Park" may record the foundation of a second park located immediately to the east of Betty Haunt Lane (pers. comm. Clive Chatters). Alternatively "Old Park" and "New Park" may refer to sub-divisions of the original park since parks were often divided by internal banks into different compartments which allowed separation of growing trees from browsing animals (Rackham 1986, 125).

In 1631 Watchingwell Park was sold by the Crown to Sir Thomas Barrington who owned the nearby manor of Swainston. A note written by Barrington at this time records his intention to fell Park Gate Wood, Round Wood, Cock Road Wood and Northwood, all within or close to the park, and describes how he intends to divide up the park into agricultural enclosures. Barrington also states his intention to retain the earthwork surrounding the park for "ye King's pale had a bank and ditches on ye outside which is not fitt to be lost" (Barrington 1631). In fact, Barrington's plans for the park were never put in to effect, for the Crown decided that the timber at Watchingwell should be preserved and therefore re-purchased the park from Barrington in 1632 (Seale ed. 1983). In 1650 the park still contained nine score deer of various sorts (Page ed. 1912, 227).

Following its final disemparkment in the eighteenth century, the former area of Watchingwell Park became the agricultural holding of Great Park. The first edition Ordnance Survey 6 inch map of 1866 shows that the area of Great Park corresponds to one of the detached portions of St. Nicholas Parish. The parish boundary clearly follows the outline of the deer park as shown on John Speed's map of 1611. To this day the northern and western sides of the park form the boundary between the modern administrative districts of Medina and South Wight. The 1985 Ordnance Survey Outdoor Leisure Map of the Isle of Wight (Scale 1:25,000) shows that the two northern corners of the park are still represented by double banks and much of the northern edge is followed by a narrow belt of woodland.

Writing of the Island in the sixteenth century, William Camden records that it had "one little forrest ... and two parkes replenished with deere, for game and hunting pleasure" (Camden 1637). The two parks mentioned by Camden are almost certainly those of Watchingwell and Wootton, which are both shown enclosed by park pales on John Speed's map of 1611. The earliest reference to a park at Wootton, owned by the Lisle family of nearby Wootton Manor, dates from 1492–3 (Page ed. 1912, 205).

In addition to the two enclosed parks John Speed also shows the whole of the Undercliff from Niton to Bonchurch as "St. Laurence Park". No park pale is shown enclosing this large area and indeed none would have been necessary, as the inner cliff itself would have formed a highly effective natural boundary. Despite its designation as a park on Speed's map, the Undercliff, with its large area of rough uncultivated ground, was more akin to a medieval chase or unenclosed hunting ground than to the relatively small enclosed deer parks at Watchingwell and Wootton.

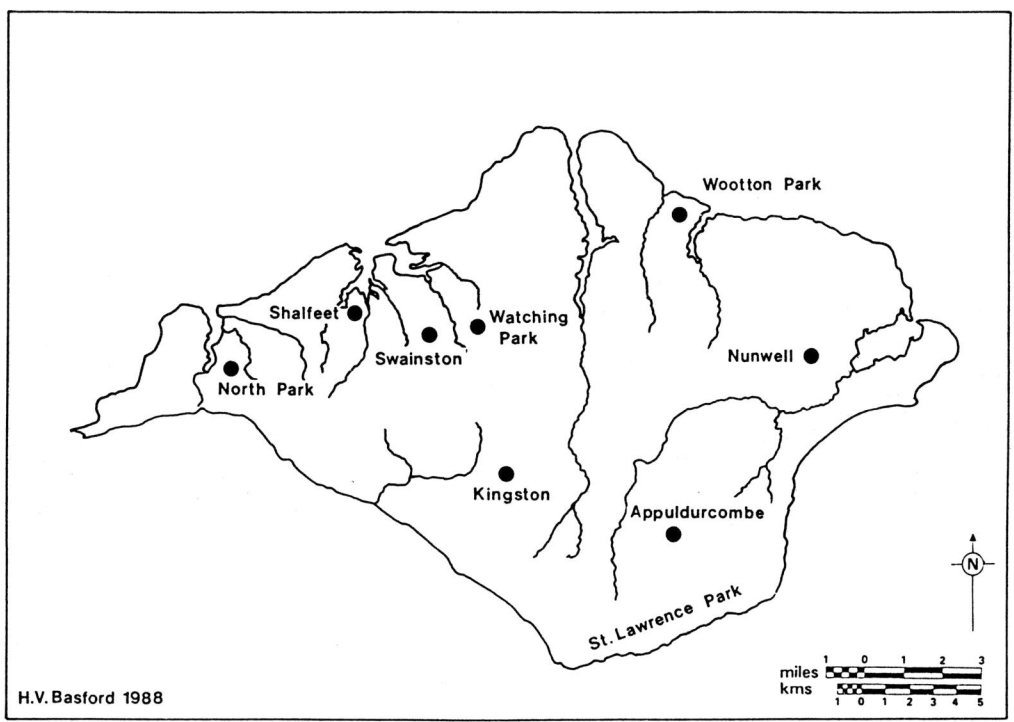

Isle of Wight Deer Parks

'Waching Park' from John Speed's map of the Isle of Wight, 1611

Situated within the Undercliff was the medieval estate of Old Park, the name of which suggests the presence of an enclosed park in this area. On the western side of the Old Park estate was a large area of rough ground known as "The Warren" in the early years of this century. Also within the estate was an enclosure known as "The Green Park" (Whitehead 1911, 248). Old Park lay within the medieval parish of Whitwell as did the adjoining estate of Woolverton, and both estates were owned by branches of the de Estur family in the thirteenth and fourteenth centuries. The ruins of a small medieval building still survive in the grounds of Woolverton Manor, near St. Lawrence, and it has been suggested that these may be the remains of a hunting lodge (Stone 1891, **1**, 132).

In addition to the parks shown on Speed's map documentary evidence exists for several other deer parks on the Isle of Wight. Henry Trenchard, who held Shalfleet Manor, appears to have possessed two parks, for in 1278 he complained that Amice, Countess of Devon, and her men broke his park of Chessell and "rescued the beasts lawfully impounded therein" and "drove off the deer from his park at Shalfleet" (Page ed. 1912, 272). An estate map of Shalfleet dated 1774 gives the name "Park Hill" to a field on the east side of Ningwood Lake.

Kingston Manor was held by the Meux family for much of the Middle Ages. In 1441 Lewis Meux and his wife Alice were granted free warren for deer and coneys in Kingston and Shorwell (Page ed. 1912, 250). They were also given licence to empark 300 acres of wood and pasture within these parishes (Shirley 1867). The place-name "Warren Hill" occurs in Kingston Parish (Kökeritz 1940). Park names occurring on the Shorwell tithe map include "Little Park", "Great Park", "Fatting Park", and "Lower Fatting Park". The two fatting park names may refer to enclosures for fattening cattle. The modern 1:10000 Ordnance Survey map includes the names "Park Lane" and "Park Lane Cottage" near Shorwell.

Swainston was an important Island estate in the Middle Ages. It was owned by the bishops of Winchester until the end of the thirteenth century and the south east wing of the house is of twelfth and thirteenth century date with remnants of the original hall and chapel. Between 1219 and 1221 rabbits and venison were transported from Swainston to bishopric residences on the mainland, indicating that the bishop had a warren at Swainston, although there is no mention of a park at this date. In 1243 Henry III ordered rabbits from three bishopric warrens in Hampshire: forty from Merdon, forty from Bitterne and a hundred from the Isle of Wight (Roberts 1988, 67–86).

By the fourteenth century the manor of Swainston was owned by the Earl of Salisbury who laid out a park there (C.P.R. 1350). Botanical evidence from Swainston also suggests the presence of parkland fairly close to the house. Lichens growing on trees in North Park Copse, immediately to the north-west of Swainston Manor, are of a type that only occur in areas that have contained mature open woodland since at least medieval times. Most medieval woodland other than that in deer parks was coppiced and therefore it is quite possible that North Park Copse was originally a wood within the deer park at Swainston (Pope 1981). However, the presence of a substantial bank and ditch on the southern side of North Park Copse shown on the Ordnance survey drawing of 1791 suggests that this copse may rather have formed part of Calbourne Heathfield which was situated to the north of Swainston Park in the sixteenth century.

Lichen evidence recorded in the last century suggests the presence of high canopy open woodland dating back to the Middle Ages at Appuldurcombe. There is no documentary evidence of a park here in medieval times when the manor was held first by the French abbey of Montebourg, which established a priory there. It is more likely, perhaps, that a park was created by the Worsley family who became the owners of Appuldurcombe in the sixteenth century after the dissolution of the monasteries. However, the earliest documentary reference to a park at Appuldurcombe dates from the early eighteenth century.

At Nunwell the lichens which have been recorded on old trees are characteristic of long standing open parkland. Once again we do not have any specific early references to a park at Nunwell. However, Sir John Oglander's remark that "of a rude chase I have now made it [Nunwell] a fit place for any gentleman" suggests that in the sixteenth century the land around Nunwell House was used as a hunting ground (Bamford ed. 1936, 84).

The most tantalising clues in our attempt to discover the positions of all the Island's medieval deer parks are provided by park place-names unsupported by any other evidence. Some of these place-names are misleading. For instance, Park Farm near Brading appears to be so called because it was once held by the de Parco family whose name was derived from their landholdings of Park Place and Little Park next to Watchingwell Park. There appears to be no evidence that Fattingpark, which constituted a detached portion of the medieval parish of Wootton, was ever a deer park. On the eastern side of Freshwater Parish the tithe map gives the place- names "North Park", "North Park Coppice" and "North Park Copse". This cluster of place-names occurs close to the parish boundary between Freshwater and Thorley and it was a characteristic of medieval deer parks that they occupied waste land on the edge of the parish. North Park Copse in Freshwater parish is a tiny area of woodland which is the only place on the Isle of Wight to contain the small-leaved lime tree, a species which is a poor coloniser and is therefore confined to ancient woodland (Spencer *et al* 1987). Place-names suggestive of medieval parkland also occur in Whippingham Parish. Only by a combination of fieldwork and documentary research, such as has been carried out in Dorset (Cantor and Wilson 1961 – 1969 and Wilson 1970 – 1978) will a complete list of the Island's deer parks ever be compiled and their boundaries defined.

EARLY GARDENS

Roman Gardens

The creation of pleasure gardens is an activity requiring both a relatively peaceful and stable society, and individuals with wealth and leisure to devote to their gardens. Such conditions did not prevail in Britain prior to the Roman occupation.

Archaeological evidence of gardens in Roman Britain is surprisingly slight but this is perhaps because the evidence has not been looked for until recently. During the excavation of Fishbourne Roman Palace, near Chichester, in the 1960's, a specific effort was made to locate garden evidence. The layout of the northern half of the formal garden was recovered and this garden has now been recreated from the archaeological evidence (Cunliffe 1971).

Reconstruction of Brading Roman Villa, showing the central open space and wall alcove

On the Isle of Wight evidence for Roman gardens might be expected to occur at one or more of the eight villas which have been discovered to date (Tomalin 1987). Most of these villas were fairly modest agricultural homesteads and it is perhaps only at Brading Villa that a sufficiently wealthy and cultured proprietor existed, able to contemplate the effort and expenditure necessary to create and maintain a pleasure garden. Excavation at Brading Roman Villa took place during the 1880's and revealed ranges of buildings and linking walls on three sides of a rectangular open space. Set within the perimeter wall, the excavators discovered a chamber of semi-circular plan which they interpreted as an alcove which "faced onto a garden" (Price and Price 1881) There is, however, some doubt as to whether this feature was contemporary with the perimeter wall; it may have been an earlier feature which had been blocked off by the wall, leaving its eastern side as a ledge projecting from the wall, and the enclosed area may have been merely a simple farmyard (Tosdevin, pers. comm.). It is unfortunate that the Brading Villa was excavated such a long time ago, as modern excavation techniques would have allowed the recovery of pollen grains and plant remains which might tell us more of the botanical history of the supposed garden at Brading.

By the late fourth century AD everyday life at Brading had deteriorated to such an extent that even a mosaic floor in the family house had been dug up to make room for a corn drying oven. The villa was now no more than a bare boards farmstead soon to be abandoned. The days of sedate country living were truly gone and with their passing the opportunity to create and tend gardens of pleasure was to be virtually banished until the later Middle Ages.

Medieval Gardens

Garden plots for the cultivation of herbs and vegetables presumably existed during the Dark Ages as they had done since prehistoric times. The earliest, and indeed the only, physical evidence of medieval gardens on the Isle of Wight which survives today, however, is at Newtown where the Bishop of Winchester laid out a new settlement in the mid-thirteenth century. Originally there were 73 burgage plots – small pieces of land each of which would have contained a house and garden. Today traces of 57 such plots survive, and may be identified by hedgerows or field banks (Basford 1980, 41–48).

Until the late Middle Ages the castle and the monastery provided the only secure environment in which the art of gardening might develop. Monastic gardens grew both medicinal and culinary herbs. Where flowers were grown it is probable that these would have had some religious significance or that they were grown for the purpose of beautifying the abbey church. Manuscripts of the time refer to "Mary Gardens" which all contained roses and the Madonna Lily, traditionally brought back by the crusaders (Fleming and Gore 1979, 17). This reference to "Mary Gardens" should not be confused with "Merry Gardens" at Lake, near Shanklin, whose name is derived from a local dialect word meaning "cherry" (Kökeritz 1940, 204). In connection with the religious significance of the lily it is interesting to note that in 1529 Quarr Abbey leased to Richard Turnewelle five gardens within the town of Newport. For each of these gardens he was to pay the ground rent due to the town and to the abbey certain odoriferous flowers called "leleys" (Hockey 1970, 208).

Only two garden references appear to have been traced which refer specifically to the Isle of Wight's most important medieval religious house, the Cistercian abbey of Quarr, near Binstead. One of these references concerns an abbey servant named John Bullock, first employed in 1492. He and his widowed mother were to live in the "Gaestn Hall" which had its own garden reaching from the north enclosure wall as far as the pond known as the "Horspole" (Hockey 1970, 212). In 1530 William Kettywell rented buildings and closes outside the south gatehouse including two "garths" (Hockey 1970, 221). These gardens, and that of John Bullock, would have been productive rather than ornamental. On the ruined walls of the abbey there grows today the wallflower *cheiranthus cheiri*. The wallflower was the symbol of faithfulness in medieval times and was deliberately grown along the walls of monasteries where it took on a religious dimension (Maclean 1981, 152–157). *Cheiranthus cheiri* does however grow on other old and undisturbed walls on the Island, such as those of the King James Grammar School at Newport (Bevis *et al* 1978, 31) and therefore the example at Quarr may not necessarily be connected with religious symbolism.

Quarr was the only abbey on the Isle of Wight in medieval times but there were also several small priories, dependent on French religious houses. The priory of St. Cross was built near the confluence of the Lukely Brook and the River Medina in the early twelfth century. Later in the same century the planned town of Newport was laid out immediately to the south of the priory. Medieval documents concerning this priory tell us of a "garden within an enclosure" where we are told money was expended for "fencing the garden" and for paying a man to "clean the dovecote". Income from the garden included 3d recovered from the sale of nettles (Hockey 1982, 49 and 52). Another religious foundation serving the town was Newport Chantry, established to provide a second priest for the growing town and to say prayers for the souls of its founders. The properties with which the Chantry was endowed on its establishment in the mid-fifteenth century included 22 gardens situated in Newport or in adjoining manors (Hockey 1982, 160).

John Speed's 1611 map of Newport shows land behind the early seventeenth century street frontage apportioned into an irregular patchwork of rectilinear plots, some of which are seemingly filled with small orchards. Immediately west of St. James' square, however, a complete block of land is given over to a segmented circular setting which is presumably the town's first formal garden. By the late seventeenth century the formal garden seems to have gained popularity amongst the citizens of Newport. The geometric gardens of this time, several of which are shown on Lea's map of 1689, betray horticultural endeavours which are clearly more ornamental than productive.

In medieval Wight the religious house next in importance to Quarr Abbey was the Priory of St. Mary at Carisbrooke. The Cartulary of Carisbrooke Priory refers to the monks' orchard and to "tithes of garden produce" but perhaps the most interesting reference concerns two acres of land at Nunwell held by the monks from Robert Oglander in return for an annual rent of one pound of cummin (Hockey 1981, 106). Cummin is a spice nowadays associated with curries, but the tenth century Glastonbury Leechdom recommends cummin for the "sufferer from hiccups" (Fleming and Gore 1979, 15).

Close to Carisbrooke Priory, on a chalk hill dominating the Bowcombe Valley and the village of Carisbrooke, stands Carisbrooke Castle, occupied for much of the earlier Middle Ages by hereditary and quasi-independent lords of the Island. The last of these hereditary rulers of the Wight was Isabella de Fortibus who carried out an extensive rebuilding programme at Carisbrooke Castle. It is at this time, and within the walls of Carisbrooke Castle, that we have the first documentary evidence of a pleasure garden on the Isle of Wight. Contemporary account rolls mention a new "arbour garden" created at the castle in the year

EARLY GARDENS

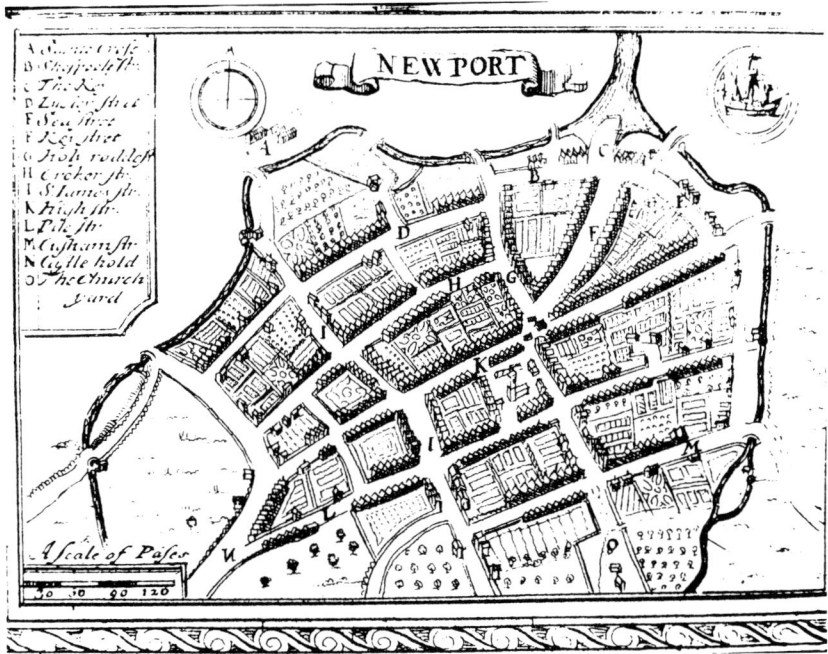

Map of Newport. Philip Lea, 1689

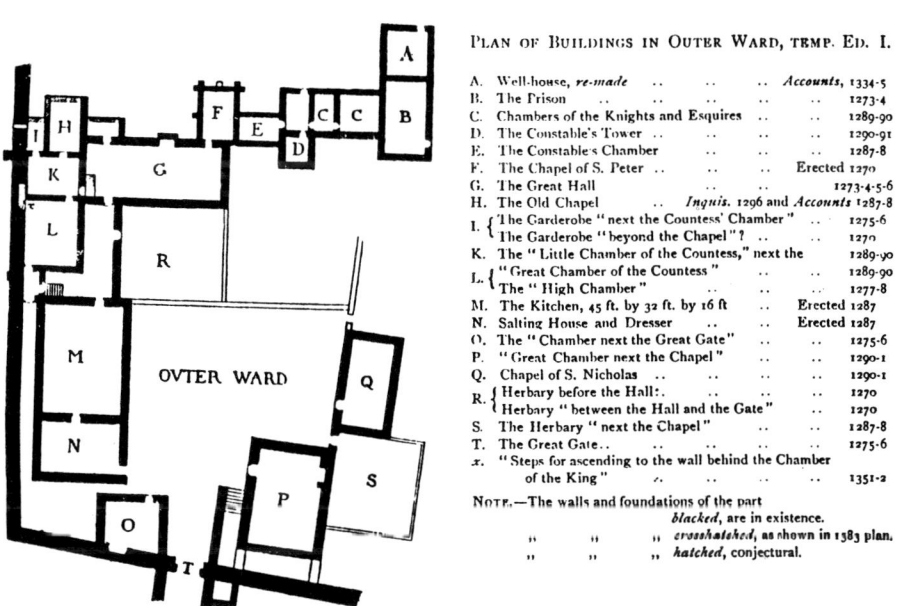

Plan of Carisbrooke Castle in the time of Edward I, showing herb gardens near the hall and chapel (Stone 1891)

1269–70. In 1270–71 the "old wall next the herbary before the hall" was pulled down and rebuilt. The setting up of a clock or sundial in the herbary is recorded between 1276 and 1286 (Stone 1891, 75). In these references the term "herbary" may be synonymous with "arbour garden" as the word "arbour" is derived from the Old English *herbere*. Originally it denoted a place for growing herbs but the word developed in meaning so that by the fifteenth century the arbour had become a garden feature consisting of a type of pergola with plants trained over a lattice to form a gallery or tunnel (Bilikowski 1983, 7). Isabella's garden was therefore perhaps a herb garden although it is tempting to imagine a tunnel-like arched arbour similar to the one recently created for the reconstructed Queen Eleanor's Garden outside the Great Hall at Winchester (Landsberg 1987).

Where was Isabella's garden situated? According to one reference quoted above it was "before the hall" and Isabella's Great Hall was the building now occupied by Carisbrooke Castle Museum. A plan of the castle as it would have been in the time of Edward I is given in *The Architectural Antiquities of the Isle of Wight* (Stone 1891, **2**, 100). This plan shows one "herbary" west of the Great Hall and another to the west of the Chapel of St. Nicholas. This second herbary near to the chapel was within the area later to be occupied by the "privy garden".

Although Isabella's herbary is the only clearly documented Island pleasure garden of the medieval period, a second such garden may have existed at Swainston. This estate was owned by the bishops of Winchester until the late thirteenth century and by the Earls of Salisbury in the fourteenth century when it possessed its own deer park. Swainston was clearly an estate of considerable substance. It seems unlikely that any other Island landowners would have possessed ornamental pleasure grounds during this period.

Just before her death in 1293 Isabella surrendered the lordship of the Island to Edward I, apparently under a certain amount of pressure. After this time the lordship of the Island was granted to royal appointees for a limited number of years or at most for a lifetime. Since the time of Isabella, therefore, the Island has lacked the permanent presence of a dominant aristocratic family, and this may have had a retarding effect on the development of the Island's houses and gardens.

Whilst the Island possesses only one or two grand mansions it does possess a wealth of manor houses on sites occupied since the Middle Ages and in many cases since Domesday. The existing buildings are mostly Jacobean or later, although some have earlier work. There are documentary references to gardens attached to medieval manor houses, including one at Gotten (Winter 1984, 61) and one at Gatcombe (Hockey 1982, 196). A document describing the widow's portion of Agnes, widow of Theobald de Gorges of Knighton who died in 1380, mentions a garden called "Purihey" with a barn and a herb garden to the south of the great hall (Hockey 1982, 197). These gardens would have been primarily functional rather than ornamental.

Medieval moated sites existed at the manors of Barton, Stenbury, Woolverton near Shorwell and Wootton. Medieval manor houses were sometimes built within a moated area and contemporary documents suggest that these moated sites often contained gardens as well as houses. Some moats may have contained only gardens, with the associated houses being nearby (Taylor 1983, 36). At Woolverton near Shorwell the site of the medieval moat lies a little way to the north-east of the surviving Tudor manor house. A geophysical survey of the area within the Woolverton moat carried out by David Motkin in 1977 indicated the presence of only a single rectangular structure in the north eastern corner of the site. Sediments dredged from the moat were significantly devoid of any sign of domestic refuse. It is possible that the medieval manor house of Woolverton may have occupied the site where the Tudor manor house now stands and that the moated site may have chiefly accommodated a garden area.

Tudor and Jacobean Gardens

The Tudor manor house at Woolverton was built in the reign of Elizabeth I by John Dingley, Deputy Captain of the Wight, and was certainly on a grander scale than the average country house (Jones 1978, 69). In front of the house is a walled forecourt with an entrance into the walled garden to one side of the house. This walled garden was described as a "pleasaunce" by the antiquary Percy Stone (1891, **2**, 137) and much of the walling still survives although it now contains only rough grass and hawthorn scrub. Walled forecourts survive also at Yaverland Manor and at Sheat Manor, whilst at Billingham Manor there is another walled garden.

The Island's grandest Tudor mansion was undoubtedly Appuldurcombe House but this building was demolished and rebuilt in the early eighteenth century by Sir Robert Worsley. Fortunately, before Sir Robert pulled down the old house he made a drawing of it and this shows the grounds to the east of the house in some detail. No main entrance is shown on the drawing so we must presume that we are looking at the garden front of the house. A paved area or terrace is shown immediately outside the house with steps leading down to a walled garden. There is a slight suggestion of a raised walk overlooking the wall on the northern side of the garden but other than that no details of the walled area are shown and indeed the space has been used for a note on the house and the derivation of its name by Sir Robert Worsley. To the south of the walled garden a bowling green is shown complete with garden roller and with gentlefolk taking a stroll on the fine turf. A note on the drawing explains that the area to the west of the bowling green was formerly a tennis court although latterly occupied by the great dining room with the library over. A curious circular building to the south of the dining room and overlooking the tennis court cannot be a gazebo or summerhouse for only a tiny entrance is shown. Its size and shape suggests that it might be a dovehouse -- still a functional as well as an ornamental feature of Tudor properties. The drawing provides no evidence of any larger grounds outside the area of the walled garden and bowling green although we have seen that botanical evidence hints at the existence of parkland at Appuldurcombe even at this early date.

Another Tudor manor house which has completely disappeared is Knighton Gorges near Newchurch. An engraving by Sir Henry Englefield shows the house perched dramatically on a mound whilst the foreground is occupied by an ornamental lake (Englefield 1816). The house survived until 1821 when it was wilfully demolished by George Maurice Bisset, the then owner (Winter 1984, 92–97). Unlike Appuldurcombe, Knighton Gorges was never rebuilt although the site of the house – a prominent natural mound – can be identified to this day. Also easily recognisable are the gate piers standing at the entrance to the grounds. The walled garden at Knighton is, however, so overgrown with trees that it has become a 'secret garden' seen by the casual passer-by as only a neglected stretch of wall. In fact this wall survives on all four sides and is probably of eighteenth century date. It may however have replaced an earlier wall. Attached to the southern side of the wall is a garden building of fairly late date, perhaps a store for orchard produce.

EARLY GARDENS

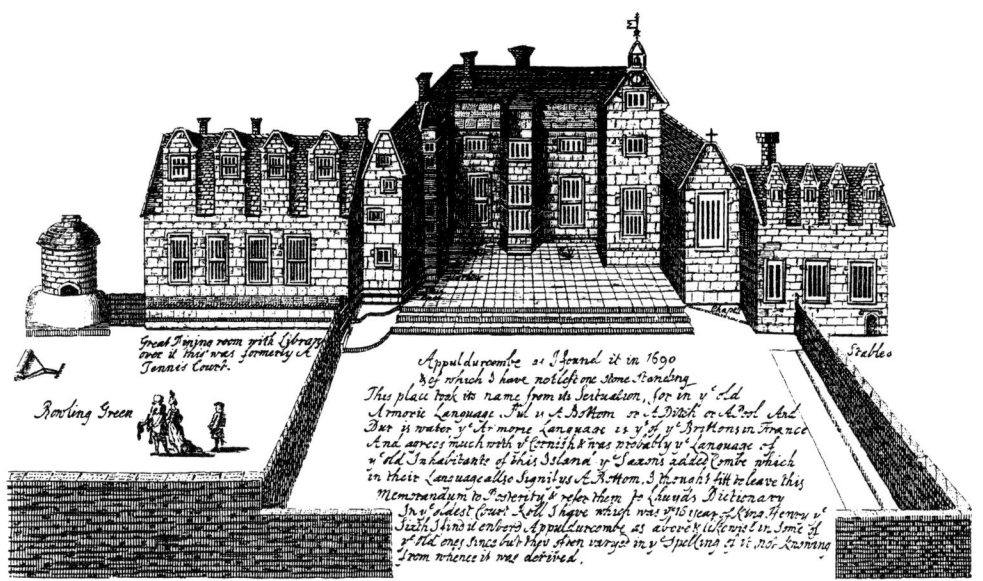

The Tudor house and garden at Appuldurcombe. Early eighteenth century drawing with notes by Sir Robert Worsley (Worsley 1781)

Late eighteenth century illustration of Knighton Gorges, showing walled garden in front of house

Within the garden an interior bank can still be discerned running right round the inside of the walls and on the eastern side a garden alcove of brick is incorporated within the bank. At the southern end of the garden a ramp of earth leads up to this raised walkway. The concept of a raised bank or walk looking out over the garden wall goes back to the enclosed gardens of the Middle Ages and was a common feature of sixteenth and seventeenth century gardens. We may therefore suppose that the garden at Knighton is older than the wall now enclosing it although parts of this wall may predate the eighteenth century. The formal plan of the garden might possibly be retrieved by careful archaeological excavation employing the methods so successfully applied to the Roman garden at Fishbourne (Cunliffe 1971) and to the gardens of Pompeii and Herculaneum (Jashemski 1979).

The main rebuilding phase for the Island's medieval manor houses fell within the first half of the seventeenth century, to which period belong Barton, Merstone, Haseley, Yaverland, Budbridge, Northcourt, Kingston, Billingham and Nunwell (Jones 1978, 70). The continuing lack of resident aristocracy was reflected in comparatively modest buildings and gardens although Northcourt was a substantial building more akin to the larger houses to be found on the mainland.

The house at Northcourt was built by Sir John Leigh in the early seventeenth century and it would seem probable that he, his son, or his grandson, originally laid out the gardens (Pinhorn 1987). Terraces surviving as earthworks in woodland to the south of the house cannot at present be confidently dated but may be attributable to the seventeenth century.

An engraving of 1796 shows a feature to the south of the house which may have been a mount. Mounts were artificial hills, usually thrown up against an outer wall so that from the top a view could be gained of the garden and the surrounding countryside (Bilikowski 1983, 9). They were distinctive features of medieval gardens but were still popular in Tudor and Jacobean times. An Elizabethan mount survives in the garden of New College, Oxford.

The Jacobean garden at Northcourt is also known to have contained a bowling green on the site of the present water garden. Close to the house is a "knot garden" created in about 1840 but reproducing a common feature of Tudor and Jacobean gardens. Early knot gardens consisted of a rectangular arrangement of beds, each compartment being filled by an intricate geometric design carried out in box or other shrubs, closely clipped into a low hedge. Sometimes herbs such as thrift were used for this purpose and infillings included flowers, low-growing shrubs and coloured gravels (Anthony 1985, 7). A "knot" forms part of the reconstructed Tudor Garden at the Tudor House Museum in Bugle Street, Southampton (Landsberg n.d.).

At Nunwell virtually nothing survives of the early garden but we have extremely good documentary and map evidence for the form and contents of this garden. Nunwell House was occupied by the Oglander family from the sixteenth century until 1980 but the Oglanders have held land in Brading since at least the beginning of the thirteenth century. The medieval manor house was at West Nunwell but in the sixteenth century a house was built on the present site. This Tudor house was almost entirely rebuilt in the first half of the seventeenth century by Sir John Oglander. A well-known character of Island history, Sir John was notable as a royalist, as a friend of Charles I and as a diarist but his interest in gardening is perhaps not so well known. In fact, his *Commonplace Book* contains quite detailed references to the garden at Nunwell. The earliest reference occurs in 1625 when he states

EARLY GARDENS

> I built the house on East Nunwell, together with brewhouse, barn, stable, Warren, gardens, orchards, Hoppegardens, bowling green and all other things thereunto adjacent in 1609
>
> (Oglander Mss.)

The interesting reference to a hopgarden is elaborated elsewhere in the Commonplace book when Sir John claims that this was the first hopgarden on the Island "made according to art" (Bamford 1936, 207). In about 1632 a more detailed description of the gardens is given which is worth quoting in full

> I have with my own hands planted two young orchards at Nunwell: the lower with pippins, pearmains, putles, hornies and other good apples and all sorts of good pears: in the other, cherries damsons and plums. In the upper garden, apricocks, mellecatoons [melons] and figs. In the Parlour Garden, in one knot, all sorts of French flowers and tulips of all sorts: some roots cost me 10d a root. In the Court, vines and apricocks, in the Bowling Green the vine and an infinity of raspberries.
>
> (Bamford 1936, 84)

Sir John also records some good advice for his descendants in his Commonplace Book

> Have a small warren for some rabbits when thy friends come. Build a pigeon-house and fit up a fishpond or two that at all times thou mayest have provisions at hand. Pale in a place to breed or keep pheasants and partridges in. I paled all my warren round about my houses in compass 12 acres.
>
> (Bamford 1936, 207)

The interest of these references is greatly augmented by the fact that a map of 1748 (Oglander 1748) shows many of the features mentioned more than a century earlier by Sir John Oglander. It is in effect a plan of Sir John's garden although there had probably been minor changes in layout during the intervening century. Several of the features mentioned in Sir John's notebooks are labelled, including "The Warren", the "Dovehouse" and the "Court". Also mentioned by Sir John and shown on the map are orchards and fishponds. Sir John made no mention of "The Prospect", an avenue of trees shown on the map running southwards from the house, so perhaps this avenue was planted after his time. The remains of a later lime avenue in the same position survive today but there are also one or two ancient limes left which apparently date from the eighteenth century or earlier.

An interesting feature of the 1748 map is that it is drawn with south at the top, unlike modern maps where north is always at the top of the page. Thus the formal gardens shown to the left of the house on the map were really on its eastern side. We have seen that Sir John Oglander refers to the "Upper Garden" and to the "Parlour Garden". These are not mentioned by name on the map but a wall is shown and perhaps divides the two gardens, the Parlour Garden presumably being the one nearest the house. Sir John states that the Parlour Garden contains "in one knot, all sorts of French flowers and tulips". This clearly refers to a knot garden. In the area presumed to be that of the Parlour Garden the word "parterre" can be read very faintly on the 1748 map. The parterre, which become fashionable in Jacobean times, was a development of the Tudor knot garden. It was made up of different shapes which were divided from one another and filled with grass, gravel, earth or flowers. The layout shown on the 1748 map as a "parterre" consists however of a series of long narrow shapes

EARLY GARDENS

Engraving of Northcourt, 1796, showing a mount or terrace to the south of the house

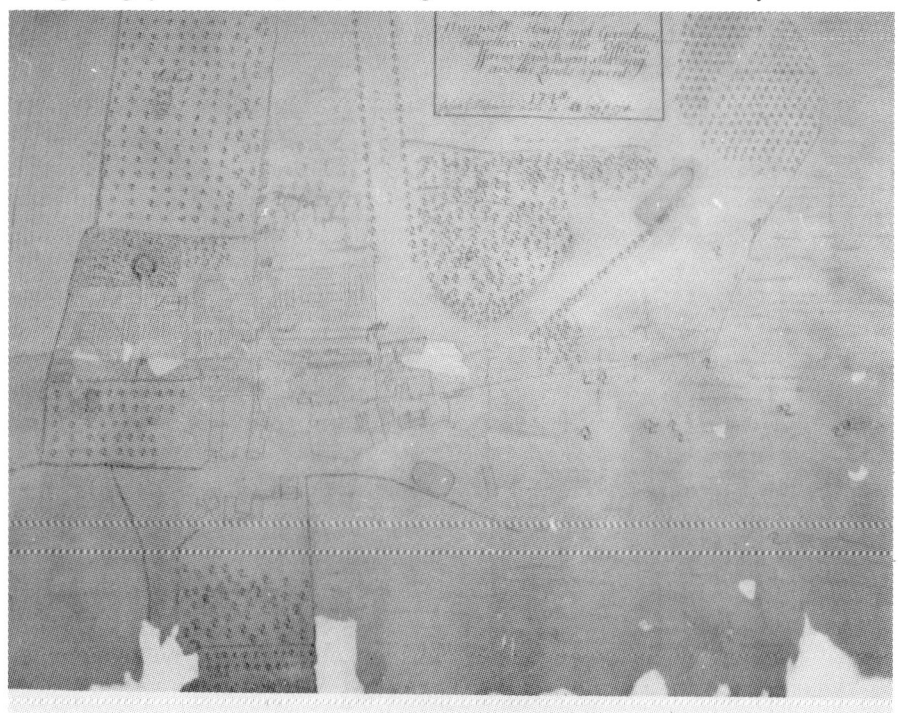

Map of Nunwell, 1748

which might be flowerbeds or ornamental terraces. The bowling green mentioned by Sir John does not appear to be labelled on the 1748 map although a large open space shown within the garden immediately to the east of the house may be the site of this feature.

There is now no trace of Sir John's formal garden to be seen at Nunwell, for it was swept away in the late eighteenth century. The only real link with Sir John's garden is provided by an area of woodland to the south-west of the house which is on the site of his "Warren", although it has been known as "The Rookery" since the nineteenth century.

In the parkland to the east of the house and gardens, a dying mulberry is the only tree which may, perhaps, be attributed to the time of Sir John. Nunwell Park is believed to have been established not later than the early seventeenth century, but most of the trees surviving are of much more recent date. Sir John records planting "above a hundred young elms and ashes, some chestnuts and serviceberries in the grove of my house" (Bamford 1936, 94) but this planting may have been in the area of the Warren rather than in the outer park to the east of the house.

We have seen that Sir John Oglander was not concerned merely with the practical and sporting aspects of his grounds. Indeed he confesses that "I have been so foolish as to bestow more money than a wise man would have done in flowers for the garden" (Bamford 1936, 94). This was the first great age of plant introduction and travellers brought back seeds and bulbs from foreign parts almost as a matter of course. Sir John mentions French flowers and also tulips which were the fashionable flowers of the time, brought from the Balkans and the Near and Middle East (Fleming and Gore 1979, 44). It is likely that Sir John Oglander was the first really dedicated amateur gardener on the Isle of Wight and it was his proud boast of the Nunwell grounds that "Of a rude chase, I have now made it a fit place for any gentleman".

LATER PARKS AND GARDENS

The Evolution of Parks and Gardens

English garden design changed considerably in the latter half of the seventeenth century under the influence first of French and later of Dutch models. The creation of the huge royal garden at Versailles by the French King Louis XIV had an enormous influence on Restoration England. The French Style incorporated elaborate parterres, water features and, most characteristically, blocks of formal woodland intersected by straight avenues and organised round a central axis. The Dutch Style was characterised by parterres, canals and orchards in a rectangular enclosure with avenues of trees projecting into farmland.

The eighteenth century was perhaps the most creative period in the history of English garden design and was marked by a movement away from formality. The first of the new eighteenth century styles has been termed the "English Forest Style" (Turner 1986) and is associated with the work of the garden designers Stephen Switzer (1682–1745) and Charles Bridgeman (1680–1738). This style is characterised by extensive plantings of forest trees and by avenues that were still regular but which lacked the excessive formality of the French Style. Charles Bridgeman has been credited with the invention of the ha-ha or sunken fence, a stone revetted ditch which allowed the grounds around the house to seem part of the wider landscape without the inconvenience of cattle straying close to the house. Slightly later in the eighteenth century William Kent (1685–1748) and Lancelot 'Capability' Brown (1715–1783) were the main exponents of what has been variously termed the 'Natural', the 'Landscape' and most recently the 'Serpentine' style (Turner 1986). 'Capability' Brown was a landscape designer who claimed to be able to see "capability for improvement" in every garden.

Towards the end of the eighteenth century, garden design came under the influence of the Romantic Movement in the arts and there was a taste for wilder scenery, both within the garden and without. The New Forest clergyman William Gilpin fostered the Picturesque style with his drawings of wild British Landscapes (Batey 1987) and his ideas were developed by Sir Uvedale Price and by Sir Richard Payne Knight.

The planned parkland advocated in the eighteenth century by 'Capability' Brown and his followers left no place for a formal flower garden immediately adjacent to the house. At the turn of the century garden designers such as Humphry Repton (1752–1818) began to reinstate these formal gardens although further away from the house informal parkland remained in vogue throughout the nineteenth century. In the Victorian era Italianate terraces were often added to an existing park.

In the nineteenth century flowering plants, which had hardly been utilised in the preceding century, became important once again. More exotic species were becoming available and garden technology was advancing, including the widespread use of heated greenhouses. The

Gardenesque style developed by J.C. Loudon emphasised the art of the gardener and the beauty of individual plants and trees rather than the layout of the grounds as a whole. 'Floral Bedding' or 'mosaiculture' also became very popular in Victorian times, utilising brightly coloured annuals arranged in geometric designs. As well as exotic plants the Victorians sometimes incorporated into their gardens exotic architectural and landscape features borrowed from European, Oriental or Egyptian design. This tradition can be traced to the interest in 'Chinoiserie' current in the eighteenth century.

Late nineteenth and early twentieth century garden design was influenced both by the idea of 'the Wild Garden' advocated by William Robinson, and by formal garden design promoted by Reginald Blomfield. The 'Arts and Crafts Movement' in garden design, as typified by the partnership of Sir Edwin Lutyens and Gertrude Jekyll, combined formal terraces and enclosed gardens with much freer informal planting schemes which placed an emphasis on herbaceous borders and a 'cottage garden' style. The gardens planned by Lutyens and Jekyll have continued to influence garden design and planting schemes throughout this century. Gardens influenced by the abstract designs of modern art are relatively uncommon in Britain but some examples do exist. Many modern gardens are 'Plantsman's gardens' where interest is focused on the plant rather than on the design of the grounds.

There are now very few gardens in Britain which predate the later eighteenth century. Such was the enthusiasm for the landscape parks designed by 'Capability Brown' and his followers that most existing gardens were completely redesigned in the new style. On the Isle of Wight there are no surviving gardens predating the later eighteenth century – merely a few isolated garden features from earlier periods. We must rely chiefly on documentary and map evidence to visualise these early gardens.

Formal Landscapes

The best evidence for the design of a formal eighteenth century landscape on the Isle of Wight is at Swainston, the home of the Barrington family in the seventeenth and eighteenth century. The layout of the grounds is clearly shown on Andrews' Map of 1769, Worsley's map of 1781 and the unpublished Ordnance Survey drawings of 1791. The 1791 six inch to one mile survey is the most detailed source and shows a walk leading northwards from the house to an area of woodland laid out with formal avenues of trees, some converging to a point. To the east of the woodland walk the natural stream is accentuated on the plan, suggesting that it had been utilised as a garden feature, and a woodland pool is shown which is still marked on the present day Ordnance Survey map. The formal woodland at Swainston appears to be a miniature example of the 'English Forest Style' and was presumably laid out in the first half of the eighteenth century. Slightly different layouts, however, are shown on Andrew's map of 1769 and the Ordnance survey of 1791, and suggest that the woodland was modified between these dates.

By 1781, when the grounds were shown on the map attached to Sir Richard Worsley's *History of the Isle of Wight*, the design might have been thought outmoded since in the later part of the eighteenth century the fashion was for naturalistic landscape parks. Sir Richard Worsley's own grounds at Appuldurcombe had recently been landscaped to the design of 'Capability' Brown, yet he viewed the layout of Swainston favourably, commenting in his History that "the pleasure grounds and walks through the woods are extensive and well laid out" (Worsley 1781, 257). Despite changes in fashion the formal woodland walks at Swainston

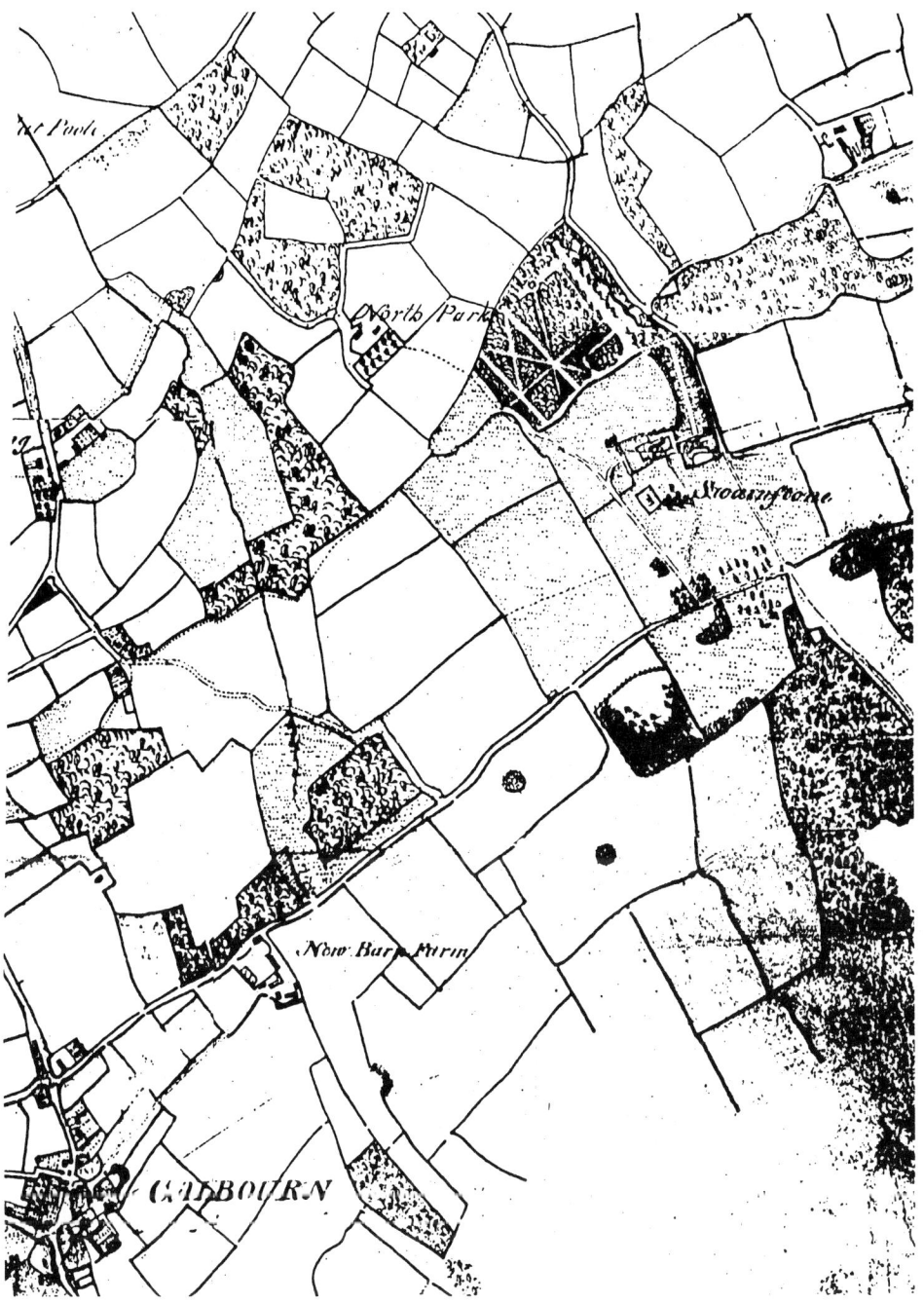

Ordnance survey plan of Swainston and North Park, 1791

survived until at least 1812 when they are shown on Clarke's *Military Marine and Topographical Survey of the Isle of Wight*.

By the 1860's no trace of the formal avenues can be seen on the Ordnance Survey six inch map although a wooded area still existed and was named "Willy Wood". Today most of the trees have been cleared from Willy Wood, but to the northwest a wooded area survives known as Lady Wood; within Lady Wood is an ornamental pond which may perhaps be the pond shown on the unpublished 1791 Ordnance survey at a point where ornamental rides converge. Lady Wood also contains the remains of a summerhouse. The floor of this feature is the only part to survive and is constructed of animal bones set vertically in the ground. The summerhouse may have been constructed during the period of 'The Picturesque' at the end of the eighteenth century. The grounds immediately surrounding Swainston Manor House are today separated from the area to the north and west of the house by a ha-ha. This feature could date from either the eighteenth or the nineteenth century.

On the 1866 Ordnance Survey six inch map, as on the earlier Ordnance drawing of 1791, it can be seen that Swainston Park extended to the south of the house and beyond the Carisbrooke – Calbourne road. Part of the area to the south of the road is clearly demarcated by a fence on the 1791 Ordnance survey. In this area there exists today an ornamental Grecian Temple which had fallen into disrepair by the early 1980's although the facade has now been restored. This may well be the same feature as the "Temple Arch" which was commissioned at Swainston in the late eighteenth century, along with various "follies" and a "gothic temple" (Tomalin pers. comm.). A brick well house known as "Winifred's Well", some distance to the east of the house, may also date from this period.

Whereas the house and grounds at Swainston retained many features of an earlier period into the nineteenth century, Appuldurcombe was more subject to the vagaries of fashion. Sir Robert Worsley was responsible for the demolition of the Tudor mansion and its replacement by a grand house in the English Baroque style between 1701 and 1712 (Boynton 1967). Until recently very little evidence has been found for any gardens created by Sir Robert and there has been a tendency to assume that the parkland surrounding Appuldurcombe was first laid out by 'Capability' Brown who undoubtedly was responsible for landscaping the grounds at Appuldurcombe in the 1770's. Nothing has been written of the earlier designed landscape surrounding the house built by Sir Robert Worsley, nor are there any earthworks suggesting the former layout of the grounds but there is, in fact, a substantial amount of evidence for these grounds although there are also many questions that cannot be answered.

The known interests and connections of Sir Robert Worsley strongly suggest that he would have taken a keen interest in the grounds of his new house. His father-in-law was the first Viscount Weymouth of Longleat, where large new formal gardens designed by George London were commenced in 1685. In 1701 or 1702 Lady Worsley wrote to her father from Appuldurcombe "I hope ... you may be able to enjoy the pleasure of your garden ... We have one no bigger than your parlour that Sir Robert is perpetually in". It is perhaps this small garden which is referred to in the Worsley account books for 1702. The entry reads "Paid William Reynolds and John Davis their bill for walling the Best Gardine Wall in Summer 1702. Ended Nov. 12 1702 £183.18.00". The sum recorded is a large one for the time and presumably refers to the creation of a pleasure garden close to the house. William Reynolds and John Davis, who built the garden wall, are believed to have been the builders of the new house at

Newtown. Street layout and surviving garden plots within the failed medieval town.

Woolverton Manor, Shorwell. Medieval moated site. Elizabethan house with walled forecourt and walled garden.

Joan Blaeu's map of the Isle of Wight, 1645, showing 'Waching Park', Wootton Park and 'St. Laurence Park'.

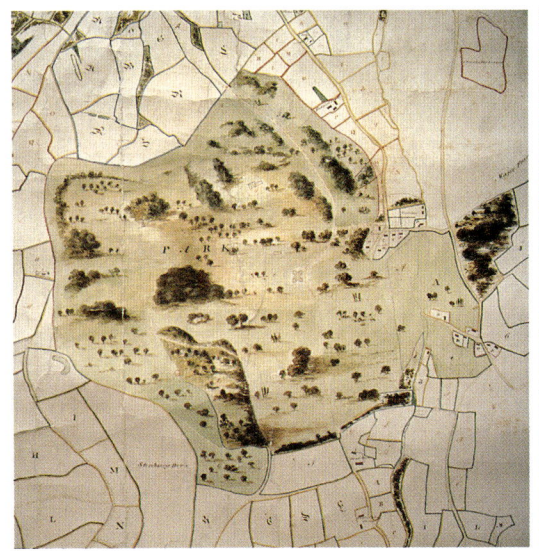

Map of Appuldurcombe Park c1800

Appuldurcombe Inner Park and Ha-ha

'The Temple', Swainston, with portico restored, 1987

Westover, from the ornamental lake

LATER PARKS AND GARDENS

Appuldurcombe (Boynton 1967, 13). An enclosed garden surrounding Appuldurcombe House to the south and west and containing rectangular flower beds is shown on Andrew's map of 1769. This may be the garden which was constructed in 1702. The Worsley account books record payments made for weeding and other garden duties at this time.

We have Sir Robert's own testimony that he was interested in gardening, for in a letter written to his brother Henry in 1717, he admits that planting was his "reigning folly" and it is known that Henry sent him rare plants from Portugal, to which country he was an envoy (Boynton 1967, 9). When first married in 1690, Sir Robert and Lady Worsley lived at their Hampshire estate of Chilton Candover where Sir Robert is known to have set out the formal gardens (Bilikowski 1987, 33). At Appuldurcombe it is perhaps significant that Sir Robert chose John James as the architect to design his new house. James was later to become Clerk of the Works at Greenwich and Surveyor at St. Paul's Cathedral (Boynton 1967, 14). More significantly, he translated d'Argenville's seminal French work *The Theory and Practice of Gardening* into English in 1712. Among the subscribers to this book were Sir Robert Worsley and his cousin Sir James Worsley of Pylewell near Lymington. It is known that James also had a practical interest in gardening (Bilikowski 1983), and it is likely that whilst working at Appuldurcombe he would have collaborated with Sir Robert Worsley to design appropriate grounds.

We have noted earlier the botanical evidence for old high canopy woodland at Appuldurcombe, but this may not necessarily indicate a medieval or Tudor deer park for which no documentary evidence has yet been traced. There is at least one piece of documentary evidence, however, which suggests that Sir Robert Worsley created the first ornamental park at Appuldurcombe in the early eighteenth century. In the Worsley account books for 1706/1707 there is an entry which reads

> James Jeffery for taking Moulds [Moles] one year ended at Michmas 1707 in the new park at Apple[durcombe] 14s.
>
> (Worsley Accts.)

Here at last is a specific mention of a park at Appuldurcombe, seemingly created at the same time as the new house.

Further evidence for an early eighteenth century park at Appuldurcombe comes from the maps of Thomas Kitchin (1764) and John Andrews (1769). Kitchin's map delineates an area around the house as parkland by means of a conventionalised park pale. No other property on the Isle of Wight has been given this parkland symbol by Kitchin. Andrews' map is much more detailed and shows a clearly defined area of shaded parkland, although the boundaries shown may not be entirely accurate. A lodge, which does not appear on later maps, is shown between the house and the northern boundary of the park. Andrews' map also depicts formal avenues of trees in the park to the west and east of the house. A further point of interest on both Andrews' and Kitchin's map is that the property to the north west of Appuldurcombe known later as Godshill Park is shown simply as "Park", implying perhaps that it had been taken out of Appuldurcombe Park at some earlier time.

In the 1770's Appuldurcombe Park was remodelled for Sir Richard Worsley who published his *History of the Isle of Wight* in 1781. In this book, Sir Richard mentions that "beeches of uncommon magnitude interspersed with venerable oaks form the background above the

LATER PARKS AND GARDENS

house". He also mentions that the park "is well stocked with deer", and he includes an engraving which shows grazing deer. One wonders whether these deer were newly imported in the 1770's or whether they had been in the park before Sir Richard's time.

Landscape Parks

When Sir Richard Worsley returned from his Grand Tour in 1772 he set about the completion of Appuldurcombe House, which had been left unfinished in 1712 due to lack of money. Sir Richard also ordered the landscape to be redesigned to complement the grandeur of the house, and in 1772 and 1781 payments of £200 and £52.10s were made to 'Capability' Brown, who is recorded as having visited Appuldurcombe in 1778 (Stroud 1950).

Appuldurcombe Park is the only landscape park on the Isle of Wight known to have been designed by 'Capability' Brown. It has been claimed that Appuldurcombe is "the only designed landscape on the grand scale on the Island" (Banks and Tandy 1980, 1) and in a very real sense this is true, for whilst the nineteenth century park at Osborne occupies a similar area it lacks the overall unity of design that is apparent in the original plan of Brown's landscape at Appuldurcombe. It should also be pointed out that the designed landscape at Appuldurcombe includes not only the area enclosed by the stone deer park wall but the "panorama of the whole valley" from Stenbury Down and Appuldurcombe Down in the west to St. Martin's Down in the east (Banks 1987, 1).

In 1773 a map of Appuldurcombe Park and the surrounding estate was drawn up by William Watts and is now preserved in the Isle of Wight County Record Office. The manuscript map shows signs of rework, suggesting amendments to accommodate changes in the layout and boundaries of the park which occurred shortly after the original drafting. The park appears to have been enlarged since 1769 (Andrew's map) along the whole of its eastern side and also to the south and west. The original boundaries can still be seen faintly on the 1773 map, suggesting that the expansion of the park took place very soon after this date. The outer boundary of the newly enlarged Appuldurcombe Park as depicted on the map was defined for much of its length by a substantially built stone wall which prevented the deer from straying. The remains of this wall survive, and parts of it have recently been repaired.

The portion of the map showing the north east corner of the park is of particular interest, for there are faint indications of some small fields which seem to have been obliterated by the expansion of the park. A Rental of the Appuldurcombe estate dated 27 March 1571 records several tenements or houses which must have been on land that was later taken within Appuldurcombe Park. The Rental specifically mentions "Freemantle Close" near the site of the later Freemantle Gate (Appuldurcombe 1571). The Watts map suggests that these houses and fields were cleared away during the expansion of the Park in the 1770's. The clearance of houses and fields – sometimes of whole villages such as Milton Abbas in Dorset – was a common feature of eighteenth century emparkment (Williamson and Bellamy 1987).

The Watts map is significantly different from Andrews' map published only four years earlier. No trace of the earlier formal garden around the house can be seen on the Watts' map: informal parkland continues right up to the house, but a walled kitchen garden is shown at the eastern edge of the park. Some areas of woodland shown on Watts' map, such as Appuldurcombe Wood and Cleveland Wood, were obviously pre-existing features deliberately retained to give an air of dignity and continuity to a gentleman's seat.

LATER PARKS AND GARDENS

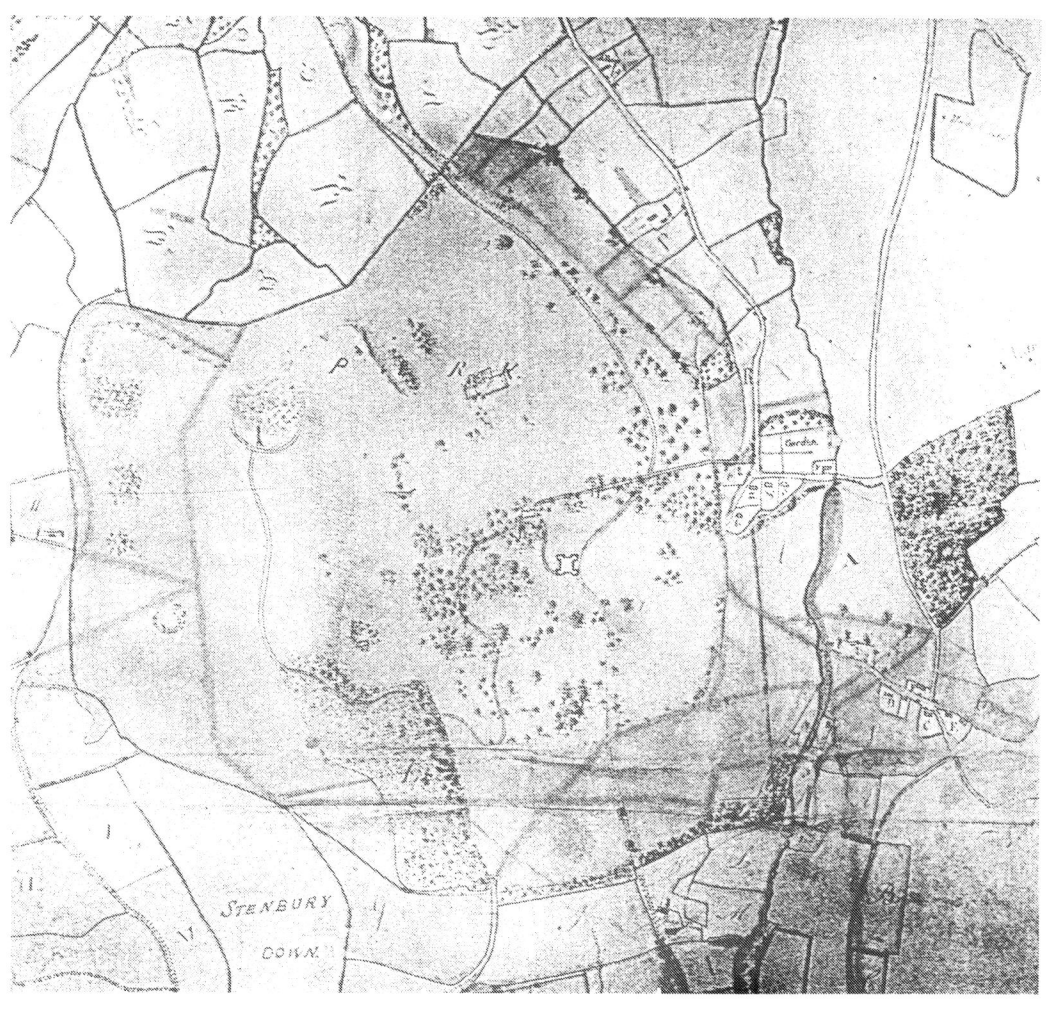

*Appuldurcombe estate map of 1773 by **William Watts**. Partially erased markings on this map suggest the subsequent expansion of the park*

LATER PARKS AND GARDENS

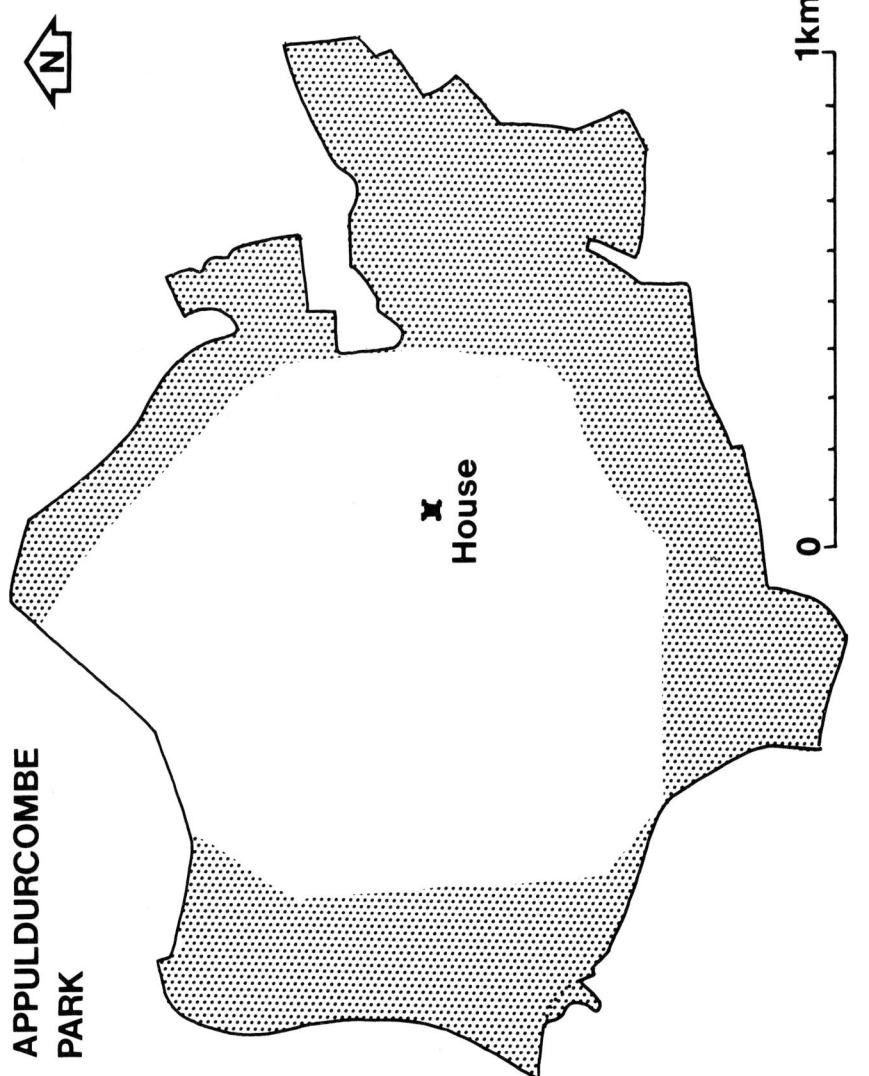

Outline plan of Appuldurcombe Park.
The stippled area represents land taken into the park by Sir Richard Worsley during the 1770's

Fernhill from the eastern side of Wootton Creek. Engraving by George Brannon

Norris Castle. Ornamental farm.

Osborne. Italianate terraces.

Nunwell. Formal Garden.

Barton Manor Garden

Urn within oriental garden, Woodlands Vale

The Temperate House, Ventnor Botanic Gardens

Vernon Square, Ryde.
A town garden in course of restoration.

LATER PARKS AND GARDENS

The Watts map of 1773 bears clear indications that, although originally drawn as an estate map, it was being used as a blueprint for the redesign of the Park. For instance, the plan depicts a 'serpentine' drive which was a typical feature of Brown's parks. The serpentine drive winds its way from the Freemantle Gate on the northern edge of the park up to the house. It then proceeds on a sinuous course through Appuldurcombe Wood and on to the 'eye-catcher' formed by the obelisk on the summit of Appuldurcombe Down. The second half of the serpentine drive has clearly been sketched-in roughly after the completion of the map, as has the obelisk itself. We know that the obelisk, designed as a memorial to Sir Robert Worsley, was built in 1774.

Another feature which appears to have been added after the initial drafting of the map is a widening of the natural stream to the east of the house. Apart from this stream, Appuldurcombe lacks the presence of water which formed an essential component of most landscape parks. There may therefore have been an attempt to create a larger body of water here. This would have added life to the valley floor and would explain the reason for the ha-ha on the eastern side of the outer park, although the water would only have been visible from the upper floors of the house (Banks and Tandy 1980).

A later copy of the 1773 Watts map, also in the Isle of Wight County Record Office, and thought to date from around 1800 shows subtle differences when compared with the original. The former boundaries of the park prior to the expansion of the 1770's are no longer visible and it looks as though tree planting had taken place in the north east corner of the park where the fields and houses are thought to have been cleared away in the 1770's. The 1800 map also suggests that further tree planting and landscaping had taken place in other areas. The widened stream on the east side of the park is still shown in outline on the 1800 map, but it is not shaded as in 1773. As no widening of the stream in this position is shown on the 1791 Ordnance survey, it may be concluded that the attempt to provide a substantial body of water within the park was unsuccessful. The existence of a waterlogged area here today, and the presence of marks on air photographs suggestive of a former pool confirm the evidence of the original Watts map that an ornamental pool formed part of Brown's landscape design for Appuldurcombe (Banks and Tandy 1980).

Appuldurcombe possessed several features which were characteristic of the landscape parks designed by 'Capability' Brown. These features included the serpentine drive and the eye-catcher formed by the obelisk on Appuldurcombe Down. The obelisk was designed to 'stop' the eye and to complete the landscape, as was "Cook's Castle" on St. Martin's Down. Despite being well outside the eastern boundary of the park, this "castle" undoubtedly formed part of the designed landscape, and is shown on the 1773 map. According to Sir Richard Worsley, writing in his *History of the Isle of Wight*, Cook's Castle was a "venerable ruin", but in fact it was a mock gothic sham, either specially built or adapted to form a landscape feature. Such fake ruins were a characteristic feature of landscape parks, although 'Capability' Brown was generally far more restrained in the use of such features than were later designers influenced by the 'Picturesque' movement.

Cook's Castle has now gone, and the recently restored obelisk is much shorter than the original monument, but the Freemantle Gate still stands in all its glory. This fine Ionic triumphal arch, with its restored wrought iron gates, marks the main entrance on the north side of Sir Richard's park. The architect is thought to have been James Wyatt, who may also have had a hand in redesigning Appuldurcombe House and who was later responsible for Norris Castle at East Cowes.

Like so many other of the landscape parks created by 'Capability' Brown, Appuldurcombe was modified in the early nineteenth century when a more private space around the house was considered desirable. The alterations at Appuldurcombe took place after the death of Sir Richard Worsley, when his niece inherited the property and in 1806 married the Hon. Charles Pelham, later Lord Yarborough. The landscape immediately surrounding the house was radically altered by the creation of an inner park at some time between this date and 1820, but the essential features of the existing landscape were carefully preserved. The boundary between the inner and outer parks was delineated by a stone wall in places, and elsewhere by an iron railing, but a ha-ha was built on the south side of the inner park to minimize the gap between this area and the outer park and to emphasise the dramatic quality of the downland rising to Appuldurcombe Wood (Banks and Tandy 1980, 17).

At Nunwell, as at Appuldurcombe, the garden fashions of succeeding generations can be traced from the seventeenth to the nineteenth century. We have seen that in 1748 the grounds at Nunwell still retained many of the features laid out more than a century earlier by Sir John Oglander. The 1748 map on which these features are shown is labelled "A Plan of Nunwell House and Gardens, Together with the Offices, Farmyard, Barns, Stabling, and the Lands Adjacent". Underneath this caption is written, in a different hand, "before ye Alterations Made in 1768, 1769 and 1778".

It was in 1768 that the east wing of Nunwell House was extended and remodelled and it is likely that alterations to the grounds were put in hand at the same time. The grounds had certainly been remodelled by 1773 when a map of the Nunwell Estate was drawn up by Samuel Donne (Donne 1773). This map shows no trace of the formal gardens to the east of the house which were depicted on the 1748 map. By 1773 these gardens had been swept away, together with the orchards and farm buildings shown on the earlier map. Parkland now extended right up to the eastern side of the house, as can be seen in the illustration of Nunwell published in Sir Richard Worsley's *History of the Isle of Wight* (1781). A walled kitchen garden to the north west of the house which has survived to the present day is shown for the first time on the 1773 map. The area of Sir John Oglander's Warren appears on this map to be unchanged apart from newly constructed stables which were later to be rebuilt by John Nash. Of the two avenues shown on the 1748 map the one running southwards from the house, labelled "The Prospect", is also shown on the 1773 map.

In the nineteenth century the necessity of an enclosed space around the house was felt and by 1866 there was a lawn on the eastern side of Nunwell House, separated from the park by a wall or fence. The terrace in front of the east wing is not shown on the 1866 Ordnance Survey 25 inch map and was perhaps constructed in the 1890's when John Oglander Glynn and his wife Florence added the balustrade to the front lawn. They also built the lodges and imported the East Lodge gates from Lake Como in Italy. Modifications to the Nunwell gardens have continued into the twentieth century, the Long Walk and Arboretum being laid out after the second world war.

The changeover from formal gardens to quasi-natural parkland in the later eighteenth century did not please everybody. Sir Henry Englefield, writing in 1816, described the parkland in front of Gatcombe House as a "dull area of weedy gravel and stunted turf" and compared it unfavourably with his ideal of a "cheerful formality of terraces and flowery beds" (Englefield 1816). The parkland at Gatcombe may have been created in the 1750's when a manor house on the medieval site was rebuilt by Sir Edward Worsley in a classical style. The

LATER PARKS AND GARDENS

COOKE's CASTLE:
An ancient Ruin on the Appuldurcombe Estate.—Isle of Wight

*The Freemantle Gate and lodge at Appuldurcombe in the early twentieth century.
The lodge is now derelict.*

LATER PARKS AND GARDENS

Engraving of Appuldurcombe Park

Detail from an engraving of Nunwell Park (Worsley 1781)

Worsley's of Gatcombe were a junior branch of the Appuldurcombe family but appear to have had equally grand ideas for the layout of their grounds.

An illustration published in 1781 in the *History of the Isle of Wight* by Sir Richard Worsley of Appuldurcombe, shows a large lake beside Gatcombe House and a yacht upon this lake. A lake of this magnificence was never created but a smaller lake shown on the 1791 Ordnance survey still exists. A small house shown by Worsley on the bank of the lake and opposite the North Front of the main House is absent from the 1791 survey. Earthworks shown in this area on the Ordnance Survey 6 inch map of 1909 suggest that Gatcombe Park may have formerly contained houses associated with the nearby village of Gatcombe.

In 1791 Gatcombe Park occupied a much larger area than it does today, stretching as far as the River Medina and Gatcombe Mill on the eastern side and nearly as far as Whitecroft to the north. The road from Chillerton to Carisbrooke ran right through the park, passing close to the eastern side of the lake, but a Gatcombe estate map of 1843 shows that the road had been moved eastwards by this time and formed the boundary of a smaller area of parkland which enjoyed greater privacy. Recent aerial photography has shown a linear soilmark in the field to the north of the lake, running northwards towards Hill Farm. This mark may represent the remains of the original road. Other soilmarks close to the linear feature may be the vestiges of tofts, or house plots belonging to Gatcombe village. If this is so, the houses must have been cleared away prior to 1791 as they were not shown on the survey of that date.

While Gatcombe Park was contracting in the nineteenth century, the park at Westover, near Calbourne, was expanding. The manor of Westover has medieval origins but the park was probably first created when Leonard Troughear Holmes purchased the estate in the 1760's and built a hunting box there. The park was recorded in 1781 when it is mentioned and illustrated in Worsley's *History of the Isle of Wight*. The illustration shows parkland to the east of the house, and the main carriage drive running along the southern side of the park. The 1791 Ordnance survey confirms that the main approach road was originally to the south of the house and shows that Westover had a relatively small area of parkland to the east of the house and an enclosed garden to the west. At the north east corner of the park the 1791 survey records the existence of the miniature lake which still provides the source of the chalk stream known as the Caul Bourne.

Westover House was largely rebuilt, possibly to the design of John Nash, in the early nineteenth century, and it was probably at this time that the park was enlarged and the main approach was re-routed to the northeast of the house. At the new main entrance to the park a picturesque lodge was built, faced with stone rubble and knapped flints. The driveway now passed alongside the lake, crossing the stream over an ornamental stone bridge which appears to have existed before the remodelling of the park. A thatched lodge known as Sweetwater Lodge is at the northwest entrance to the park, on the Calbourne–Freshwater road and is of early nineteenth century date. Further to the west along this road is another picturesque estate dwelling, Wheelbarrow Cottage.

The landscaping of the Westover Estate seems to have involved the planting of many copses, plantations and shelter belts outside the park itself. These included Westover Plantation along the slope of Westover Down, a belt of trees lining the Calbourne–Brighstone road along the eastern boundary of the park and Sweetwater Copse running southeast from the western lodge to Westover Copse.

LATER PARKS AND GARDENS

The 1866 Ordnance Survey 6 inch map shows a much larger area of parkland at Westover than was shown on the 1791 survey, and the area immediately around the house is shown as an inner park or pleasure ground, heavily planted with ornamental trees except in the area occupied by the walled kitchen garden. Today a ha-ha still defines part of the lower park in front of the house.

Like Gatcombe and Westover, Osborne was in origin a medieval estate and would in the early eighteenth century have had a manor house of vernacular design. The owner of the estate in the later eighteenth century was Robert Pope Blachford who succeeded to a fortune which allowed him to rebuild the house and to practise the fashionable art of landscape gardening. He was responsible for creating the first park at Osborne in the 1770's. This park was centred on the valley which runs north-eastwards from the house to the sea. Blachford also laid out pleasure grounds and built a walled kitchen garden. A feature of the new park was the ha-ha separating the house, stables, pleasure grounds and kitchen garden from the outer park. An engraving by Barber shows the house built by Blachford and the surrounding park just before the rebuilding of the house and alterations to the grounds carried out by Queen Victoria and Prince Albert. Deer are shown in the park although there is no other evidence for deer at Osborne. It is known, however, that the park was grazed by horses, cattle and sheep (Phibbs *et al* 1983). Osborne as rebuilt by Blachford received a favourable mention in Worsley's *History of the Isle of Wight* published in 1781.

Engraving of Osborne House and Park before the alterations carried out by Queen Victoria and Prince Albert

LATER PARKS AND GARDENS

Engraving of Gatcombe Park (Worsley 1781)

LATER PARKS AND GARDENS

Much of our information about eighteenth century landscape parks comes from Worsley's *History*, which describes the homes of the local gentry and includes engravings of some of the more important landscape parks and pleasure grounds. The map of the Isle of Wight at the end of the book shows twenty-eight parks and can be studied in conjunction with Andrews' map, published in 1769. The two maps of Andrews and Worsley depict not only the more substantial landscape parks but also a number of smaller parks and pleasure gardens. In West Medine, grounds shaded on the maps include Afton, Alvington, Billingham, Brook, Northcourt and Sheat: in the East Medine, grounds so identified are Appley, Barton, Fairlee, Padmore, Pidford, The Priory, Standen and Staplers.

Worsley praised the gardens at Northcourt as being well laid out and commanding an extensive view of the sea. In 1795 Northcourt came into the possession of Richard Bull, M.P. who, together with his daughter Elizabeth, had an "enthusiasm for landscape gardening". During Bull's ownership a mausoleum, a conservatory, a dairy, an alpine bridge, a Temple of the Sun and a rustic summerhouse were erected (Pinhorn 1987). The summerhouse appears to have been sited to the north of the house in the area known as The Dell, where a building and a monument are marked on the Ordnance Survey 1862 25 inch map. The floor of a summerhouse can still be seen in The Dell and like that of the summerhouse at Swainston, this floor is constructed from animal bones. The alpine bridge was presumably the one across the Shorwell–Carisbrooke road which has been recently rebuilt. The Temple of the Sun appears to have been situated to the east of the road in the wooded area known as Mount Ararat, where the 1862 map shows a building on a mound. The mound can still be seen today, as can terraces within this area. These may be the result of landscaping carried out by the Bull family.

The gardens of Barton Manor in 1776 included formal terraces, shrubberies, a wilderness, ponds and a mount (Phibbs *et al* 1983). Barton Manor was adjacent to the Osborne Estate and in the eighteenth century it was still owned by Winchester College who let it out on long leases, one of which, in 1785, was to Robert Pope Blachford of nearby Osborne. In the 1840's, Barton was purchased by Victoria and Albert as an extension of the Royal estate at Osborne and a model farm was built, much of which still survives (Pinhorn 1987). In the early years of the twentieth century the gardens were remodelled by King Edward VII, but many of the eighteenth century features were retained. In the 1960's a skating pond, once used by Queen Victoria, was converted into a water garden.

The Priory, a coastal property north of St. Helens and named after the nearby medieval priory, was praised by Worsley who commented that

> the situation is remarkably pleasant and the gardens are laid out with taste.

The grounds were well wooded and contained

> winding walks ... supplied with suitable seats for the enjoyment, through well contrived vistas, of a prospect that boasts of particular beauties
>
> (Cooke 1808)

The 1825 edition of Brannon's *Vectis Scenery* includes an engraving of the Priory grounds and shows the picturesque remains of the old watch tower which stood on Nodes Point at the southern end of Priory Bay. This ruined tower seems to have been retained within the Priory grounds as an ornamental feature.

LATER PARKS AND GARDENS

The Growth of the 'Picturesque'

The large numbers of Tours, Guidebooks and Descriptions of the Isle of Wight which began to appear in the last decade of the eighteenth century are just as important as early maps in the study of Island parks and gardens. Many of these books contain engravings which are a valuable source of information on the layout of parks and gardens at this period. The guidebooks of this time catered for the growing numbers of upper-class tourists who were now visiting the Island. These travellers were influenced by the Romantic Movement in literature and the arts and had a taste for picturesque scenery. This taste was fostered by writers such as William Gilpin, a New Forest clergyman who pioneered the study of British landscapes and whose ideas stimulated a new movement in garden design – the Picturesque (Batey 1987).

Gilpin published a book about his tour of the West Country and the Isle of Wight in 1798 which contained favourable comments regarding Appuldurcombe where he noted that "the grounds ... are laid out in a style of greatness equal to the mansion" (Gilpin 1798). Perhaps Appuldurcombe appealed to Gilpin because the downs surrounding the park gave it a more rugged appearance than many of the other landscapes designed by 'Capability' Brown, which were really idealised versions of the gentle scenery of southern England. With regard to Isle of Wight scenery in general, Gilpin stated that "We ... found ourselves rather disappointed in the chief object of our pursuit, which was the picturesque beauty of its scenery".

The Romantic Movement stimulated an interest in medieval times, and architects began to design houses in the gothic style which had been out of favour since the end of the Middle Ages. Fernhill was one of the first Island houses to be built in this style. It was constructed at the end of the eighteenth century for Thomas Orde Powlett, Lord Bolton, Governor of the Isle of Wight, on a new site near Wootton. In his *Tour to the Isle of Wight* published in 1796, Tomkins refers to a "Druids' Temple" in the grounds of Fernhill. A few years later the surrounds of Fernhill were described very admiringly:

> The grounds rank amongst the finest in the Island, the shrubbery extending to Wootton Bridge and the plantations throughout are flourishing and luxuriant. The arbutus abounds here in perfection and various tender and exotic plants are to be found thriving amongst the sheltered walks.
>
> (Cooke 1808)

The house at Fernhill was destroyed by fire in 1938 and the grounds were no longer maintained. The remains of the ornamental carriage drive and a curious circular walled garden have recently been studied by local botanist Mr. Bill Shepard who has found that even after fifty years of neglect exotic shrubs remain in the drive which may be descended from those planted in the late eighteenth century.

Many of the dwellings and pleasure grounds inspired by the Picturesque Movement were on a much smaller scale than Fernhill. There was a taste for rustic simplicity and several cottages ornées were built which were designed for gentlemen to live in, as opposed to the quaint lodges adorning parks such as Westover which were occupied by estate workers.

Sandham Cottage was the property of John Wilkes, a colourful and eccentric political character who spent his last years on the Isle of Wight. The site of his cottage, in Sandown High Street, is now occupied by more recent development. Wilkes devoted much time to the layout of his grounds, but they did not merit the approval of one late eighteenth century writer:

> The taste shown by him in ornamenting his rooms and grounds bore a great affinity to that displayed in his person . . . all was overdone and gaudy, the very reverse of chaste simplicity.
>
> (Baker 1799)

Devotees of the Picturesque enjoyed dramatic scenery and it is no accident that the Undercliff became the home of several wealthy settlers in the latter part of the eighteenth century. One of the first of several cottages ornées to be constructed in the Undercliff was Steephill Cottage, built for another Governor of the Isle of Wight, Hans Stanley, about 1770. There is an engraving of the cottage and its grounds in Worsley's History of 1781. Tomkins illustrates a viewpoint overlooking the grounds of Steephill Cottage which consisted of

> . . . a curious rock called the Devil's Bridge. In a chasm of the rock is placed a seat, the approach to which is by a rude flight of steps. From this situation you overlook the house and grounds, and have a full sea view.
>
> (Tomkins 1796)

The gardens of Steephill Cottage are described in some detail by Cooke

> . . . a bubbling crystal spring replenishes a capacious hollowed stone, carved as a scollop shell, giving a delicious coolness to the apartment and the surrounding lawn . . . Above on the right, rises the garden, on a broad terrace, sheltered by the rocky rampart, amongst whose detached fragments are some romantic seats and a pleasing hermitage lined with moss. Other springs, alike cool and pellucid, adorn and refresh the different walks and form beautiful cascades.
>
> (Cooke 1808)

St. Boniface Cottage at Bonchurch was another 'gentlemanly' cottage which must have been built at a fairly early date since Worsley (1781) comments approvingly that "Colonel Hill . . . has made considerable additions there and the garden is laid out with taste".

Worsley himself was to succumb to a taste for the picturesque but perhaps of equal importance in his choice of a rustic retreat was a desire for seclusion from the public gaze. Following his disastrous divorce in 1782 Sir Richard travelled abroad until 1797. After his return to England he was preoccupied with his important art collection at Appuldurcombe but he also spent much of his time with his 'housekeeper' Mrs. Smith at Sea Cottage, which was near to St. Lawrence in the Undercliff and close to Steephill Cottage. In the grounds of Sea Cottage and the adjacent property of Lisle Combe, which belonged to his mother, Worsley built several classical temples, one of which remains, and he planted a vineyard which was not successful (Boynton 1967). Near to the coast at Sea Cottage was a small artillery platform or battery on which were mounted guns said to have been cast during the French Revolution. Although written after Worsley's death, a description of the grounds at Sea Cottage published by Barber in 1834 is worth quoting

> the late Sir Richard Worsley fitted up this villa in a style worthy of his refined taste and adorned it with a gateway by Inigo Jones, brought from Hampton Court, a pavilion designed from the Temple of Minerva at Athens, a little temple called the Seat of Virgil, ornamented with a bust of that poet, and a Grecian greenhouse, copied from the Temple of Neptune at Corinth. Of these, the pavilion and greenhouse only remain; and most of the pieces of virtu formerly collected here are now at Appuldurcombe. The grounds are not extensive but are

laid out with much taste, and with a judicious care to take all possible advantage of the picturesquely varying surface.

Sea Cottage later became known as Marine Villa and then as St. Lawrence Cottage. It is now divided into two properties. Terraces survive in the garden, set out on the hillside leading down to the sea (Bilikowski 1986). The grounds contain the little gothic shrine known as St. Lawrence Well which formerly stood by the road until this was re-routed to the north in the later nineteenth century. The adjacent property of Lisle Combe was enlarged and remodelled by Lord Yarborough in the early nineteenth century to form a large cottage ornée set in spacious grounds. In the twentieth century Lisle Combe was the property of the poet Alfred Noyes who described the gardens in his book *Orchard's Bay* (Noyes 1939).

Also in the Undercliff just south of Niton village is Puckaster Cottage, built at some time between 1812 and 1824. It was described by George Brannon as a

> beautifully designed cottage belonging to James Vine Esq. . . . The sea-front is an elegant semi-circle with an overhanging thatched roof, supported by the trunks of trees entwined with flowering plants – which also climb . . . about the walls.
>
> (Brannon 1824)

Sea Cottage, St. Lawrence. Later known as
Marine Villa or St. Lawrence Cottage. Engraving by George Brannon

Puckaster today retains small pleasure grounds typical of an early nineteenth century cottage ornée. The garden spills down the hillside from the house in a series of terraces. There is a circular shrubbery walk, a walled garden and a small exotic garden with palms. Steps lead through rustic stone archways down the cliff to Puckaster Cove (Bilikowski 1986).

Another Undercliff property which possessed notable gardens in the early nineteenth century was "The Orchard", situated slightly to the east of Puckaster Cottage. This formed the summer retreat of General Sir Willoughby Gordon. The grounds were illustrated by Brannon who described them as

> narrow, steep, walled terraces, clothed with a profusion of the choicest fruit trees, which flourish with great luxuriance, and the coping is embellished with a number of handsome flower vases and other appropriate decorations
>
> (Brannon 1824)

Immediately to the east of "The Orchard" is the property known as "Mirables". The estate is of medieval origin (Whitehead 1911) and although the present house is Victorian it incorporates earlier work. A detailed plan of the gardens at Mirables, dated 1791, is preserved at the Isle of Wight County Record Office. In 1808 the grounds were described with characteristic enthusiasm by William Cooke

> ... a lawn, gently declining to the shore ... is surrounded by a shrubbery, intersected by serpentine walks, enriched by a profuse display of flowers and cooled by a crystal stream of ever flowing water. The pleasure grounds altogether are but of small compass, but so contrived as to appear of considerable extent. The walks under the cliff in particular are wildly romantic ...
>
> (Cooke 1808)

The northern coastline was also considered picturesque and contained a number of cottages ornées and marine villas by the early nineteenth century. Binstead Parsonage, built before 1808, was a small thatched cottage immediately south west of Binstead Church, and had wooded grounds stretching to the shore. Barber mentions "an assemblage of knolls and lawns, flowerbeds, elegant shrubs, noble evergreens, rockwork" and a "delightful rustic summerhouse". He also describes a terrace "looking out on the Solent through umbrageous trees" (Barber 1834).

In 1824 George Brannon published *Vectis Scenery*. This work included "A New Map of the Isle of Wight", which claimed to show all the principal "Seats and Villas". In the earlier maps of Andrews and Worsley, most of the properties identified by name were set in rural parkland and were the homes of local gentry. Many of the newer properties shown by Brannon, however, were marine residences belonging to members of the upper classes, who had their principal homes elsewhere. Several of these properties were clustered around Ryde which had been developed during the eighteenth century by the Player family. People of position had settled in the town by the early nineteenth century. Members of the nobility such as the Duke of Buckingham, Earl Spencer and the Hon. Charles Anderson Pelham all had villas close to the sea, surrounded by tasteful if not extensive grounds. To the west of the town George Player lived at Ryde House which was set within a moderately sized park. To the east of the town there was a string of marine residences, such as St. Clare, Puckpool, Fairy Hill and Sea Grove, all of which were set within their own grounds.

LATER PARKS AND GARDENS

The Influence of Repton and Nash

Adjoining Ryde on the east was the estate of St. John's where Colonel William Amherst built a house about 1769. Edward Simeon purchased the estate in 1796 and from 1797 onwards he remodelled the grounds and laid out a park. Humphry Repton was the designer, a fact that is stated in a contemporary guidebook, (Britton and Brayley 1804). Repton was accustomed to present his proposals in a "Red Book", so called because of its binding, in which he included watercolours of the landscape before and after his improvements. Unfortunately the whereabouts of the Red Book for St. John's cannot be traced, but some idea of Repton's layout can be gained from an estate map of 1803 in the Isle of Wight County Record Office.

Repton's work at St. John's involved the removal of hedge boundaries to create a parkland setting and the creation of a new approach through plantations to the house. At the entrance he built two clematis-covered thatched lodges which are illustrated in Cooke's *New Picture of the Isle of Wight* (1808). These lodges seem to have been demolished towards the end of the nineteenth century. There was also a "Marina", an ornamental building designed for bathing and viewing the seascape. This was illustrated and described by Cooke in the following terms: "Under the slope of the grounds, which have much the appearance of a park, appear the woods, in front of which stands the Marina, a pretty Gothic or Moorish castle". This building appears to have been demolished during the nineteenth century.

Classical lodge to Northwood Park, designed by John Nash. This building was demolished in 1939

The St. John's estate remained intact only until the mid- nineteenth century when land was sold for building developments (Bishop Lovett 1979). In 1865 Sir John Simeon sold the remaining undeveloped portion of the estate by auction, and St. John's House itself was sold with just 16 to 20 acres of grounds, compared with the original estate of 313 acres. In 1871 the house and grounds were again sold to John Peter Gassiot who called in the landscape gardener W.B. Page of Southampton to redesign the grounds. It was probably at this time that the new St. John's Lodge was built at the south east entrance to the greatly reduced grounds. This lodge still survives as a listed building and St. John's house is now occupied by Bishop Lovett Middle School. The grounds today appear to retain some features relating to their remodelling by W.B. Page in 1871. Within a former shrubbery walk which encompasses the grounds, the remains of a seven sided mock gothic folly, a rusticated grotto, rock gardens and a water garden may still be seen.

Between the years 1796 and 1802 Humphry Repton was in partnership with the architect John Nash, famous today for the design of London's Regent's Park and Regent's Square and also responsible for the Royal Pavilion at Brighton. In 1798 Nash started to build East Cowes Castle as his own Isle of Wight residence and it is thought that Repton designed the grounds. Repton's drawing of the castle was reproduced in Peacock's *Polite Repository* for November 1800 and since his engravings in this almanac were nearly always of places which he had improved, the implication is that he devised "the plantations of elm and beech, the banks of rhododendrons and azaleas, which fringe the grassy slopes and winding paths of Nash's pleasance" (Stroud 1962, 106).

It may well have been while he was visiting East Cowes Castle that Repton was invited to design grounds at Norris for Nash's neighbour, Lord Henry Seymour. At this time Norris Castle was being built for Seymour to designs by James Wyatt. Like the nearby East Cowes Castle, this was in the gothic style although rather more restrained and authentic than Nash's building. There is no reference to a Red Book ever having been produced by Repton for Norris Castle but modern research indicates that he was responsible for the layout of the grounds (Carter *et al*, 1982).

In 1799 James Wyatt designed an ornamental farm at Norris in the form of a Norman castle with embattled walls (Fowler 1983). The ornamental farm, or ferme ornée, had been part of the English landscape gardening tradition since the mid-eighteenth century when William Shenstone had turned his farm, the Leasowes near Halesowen, into a work of art (Thacker 1979, 199–203). Another ferme ornée, at Fairy Hill, near Ryde, is known to have existed by 1804 (Britton and Brayley 1804).

Across the river from the newly built Norris and East Cowes Castles, the estate of Bellevue in West Cowes had been purchased by the financier George Ward in 1793 and renamed Northwood Park. Ward had dealings with John Nash for many years and it is known that Nash was responsible for the tower of St. Mary's Church which stands in the grounds of Northwood Park. Nash also designed the Doric lodge alongside the church and a second classical lodge which stood at the junction of Park Road and Terminus Road until it was demolished in 1939 (Caws and Brinton 1983). At the southwest entrance to the park stands the picturesque Debourne Lodge and across the road from this is The Round House, which was probably a toll-house on the Ward estate. It has recently been shown (Temple 1987) that these two structures were almost certainly the work of George Repton, one of Humphry Repton's

LATER PARKS AND GARDENS

The Manor,
Near Ryde, Isle of Wight

EAST COWES CASTLE,
The Seat of John Nash, Esq.
ISLE OF WIGHT

architect sons, who worked for Nash after the partnership between the architect and his father had been dissolved about 1802 and continued in the practice until after 1820 (Summerson 1935). Presumably the grounds at Northwood Park were landscaped soon after their purchase although they may have been modified when the house was rebuilt in 1837 to a design by James Pennethorne. Pennethorne was an adopted son of Mrs. Nash, and Nash's successor in the architectural practice. The main carriage drive to the rebuilt house entered from the distant south west corner of the Park at Debourne Lodge, no doubt in order to impress the visitor during his long journey through the park to the classical walled forecourt where he would alight from his coach. Despite this grand approach Brannon was not impressed with the park in 1837, claiming that it was "deficient in those sylvan honours which might be expected from its bearing so promising a designation" (Brannon 1837). There are certainly beautiful trees at Northwood Park today, despite much housing development and the Great Storm of 1987. It is also possible to trace the entire boundary of the park, the stone walls of which have been preserved by covenant.

The Royal Park of Osborne
The northern coast of the Isle of Wight was known to the young Queen Victoria who had spent holidays at Norris Castle as a child. In the early 1840's she and Prince Albert were looking for a family home in the country. In 1843 Osborne was put on the market by Lady Isabella Blachford and in 1845, after a trial visit, it was purchased by Victoria and Albert. Various adjoining estates, including Barton, were also purchased in 1845 and in the following years to ensure total privacy and to allow Albert to pursue his interests in agriculture and forestry. Albert was closely involved with the design of the new house at Osborne, built by Thomas Cubitt, and with the landscaping of the grounds. The Prince does not seem to have employed a professional landscape designer, although he consulted his artistic adviser, Ludwig Grüner, on the garden layout (Charlton 1986). Albert greatly admired the art and architecture of Italy and compared the view over the Solent to that of the Bay of Naples. The new house was intended to resemble an Italian villa and garden terraces were constructed on its seaward side. From the top of the Flag Tower on the recently completed Pavilion Wing Albert supervised the grading and planting of the terraces, using signal flags to direct the workmen (Jones and Jones 1987, 122).

In the layout of the grounds Albert retained elements of the late eighteenth century Blachford design. The pleasure grounds and walled kitchen garden in front of the house were preserved although the ha-ha which had enclosed this area was filled in. The area of parkland was considerably enlarged, the Great Avenue and other drives were laid out and a boundary belt was planted on the western side to give greater privacy.

As a designed landscape Osborne lacks the coherence and unity achieved in the designs of Brown, Repton and their followers. A recent survey has demonstrated that Prince Albert was as much concerned with utility and the desire for privacy as with aesthetic considerations, although these were undoubtedly important (Phibbs *et al* 1983). Albert was also constrained by the decision to retain the old Osborne House whilst the Pavilion Wing of the new building was being constructed, with the consequence that the Pavilion, intended as the Royal Family's private wing, does not overlook the centre of the valley which forms the core of Osborne Park.

The real importance of Osborne is that it is in many ways so typically Victorian in its garden design, plantings and organisation. Whilst the outer park was planted mainly with deciduous trees, the grounds between the house and the Prince of Wales Lodge contained evergreen shrubberies and exotic specimen evergreen trees planted singly. Many of these were memorial trees (Phibbs *et al* 1983, 57). The widespread planting of specimen trees in Victorian gardens reflects a growing interest in the characteristics of individual plants This contrasts with eighteenth century planting schemes which valued trees and plants mainly for their contribution to the overall design.

The Italianate terraces were typical of Victorian garden design although the irregularity of the Osborne terraces, dictated by the slope of the land, was somewhat unusual. The balustrades, steps, urns, statuary and fountains which decorated the terraces were features to be found at many other gardens designed in this period. The displays of massed floral bedding on the terraces were a famous style of Victorian planting design (English Heritage 1987).

Exotic architectural embellishments, such as the Chinese house at Shugborough in Staffordshire, were not an unknown element in eighteenth century gardens but became more common in the Victorian period. Typical examples include the Pagoda fountain at Alton Towers, the Chinese and Egyptian gardens at Biddulph Grange and the alpine garden in the Edinburgh Royal Botanic Garden. The Swiss cottage at Osborne is very much part of this tradition, although in this case an authentic building, rather than a purpose- built copy, was erected.

The kitchen garden played an important part in the economy of the Victorian Country House, supplying fresh fruit and vegetables in and out of season. The technically-minded Victorians used the latest horticultural methods to 'force' produce for the table. Greenhouses were important to raise the large number of exotic annuals required for 'bedding out'. At Osborne the walled kitchen garden constructed for the Blachfords in the late eighteenth century was retained and the entrance portico from the earlier Osborne House was added to the east wall in about 1848. Within the kitchen garden are two greenhouses considered to be by the Metallic Hot House Manufactory of Birmingham, dated to 1854, and modelled on similar greenhouses at Frogmore in Berkshire (English Heritage 1987).

The great value of Osborne is that it remains so little changed. Despite the use of the grounds by the Royal Naval College in the early twentieth century and much additional planting by the Forestry Commission, Osborne has preserved intact the essential features of Albert's design and the parkland has survived more completely than in any other major landscape park on the Isle of Wight.

New Parks and Gardens of the Nineteenth Century

New parks continued to be created throughout the nineteenth century, as well as large numbers of gardens substantial enough to be shaded on the 1866 6 inch Ordnance Survey map. The West Wight was an area that had contained few gentlemen's residences in the eighteenth century, but several parks were in existence by 1824 when Brannon's map was published. The 1791 Ordnance survey shows Norton Lodge on the coast immediately across the river from the town of Yarmouth, but no park existed there at that time. By 1808 the park had been laid out and William Cooke remarked that "a beautiful garden surrounds the house ... and a light park paling incloses the grounds" (Cooke 1808). Cooke makes no mention of Westhill, a property to the west of Norton Lodge with somewhat smaller grounds, but Westhill is shown on Brannon's map in 1824. During his tour of 1808 Cooke passed Farringford Hill, just to the

LATER PARKS AND GARDENS

west of Freshwater Bay, where he described and illustrated a "newly erected edifice ... the residence of Mr. Rushworth".

Many years later, in 1853, Farringford was to become the home of the poet Alfred Lord Tennyson and his family. By that time a small park existed but Tennyson made a number of improvements to the grounds. He cut broad glades through copses to the north and south of the house and laid out a lawn. In 1860 a lodge was built opposite the entrance to the Park. A sunken fence or ha-ha was constructed between the park and the garden, and a stone summerhouse was built in "The Wilderness" (Tennyson 1976). The Farringford gardens were linked with The Wilderness, which lay on the southern side of Green Lane, by a wooden footbridge.

From many references to the gardens and park at Farringford in the Journal of Emily Tennyson (Hutchings and Hinton 1986) it is clear that both she and the poet derived great pleasure from their grounds and from practical gardening. "Planting potatoes" and "sweeping leaves" might be considered rather eccentric activities for a Victorian gentleman who would more usually have confined himself to the planting of ornamental features such as the "Fernery" recorded by Emily. In 1864 a Wellingtonia tree was planted at Farringford by Garibaldi, the Italian nationalist, who was staying at nearby Brook House with the Seely family. Garibaldi also planted an oak tree at Brook which still survives, although the Farringford Wellingtonia is now dead. At Brook Garibaldi would have observed the park that had recently been improved and enlarged by the Seely's.

A completely new park was laid out at Wydcombe, near Niton, before 1862, around the greatly altered manor house. This was the creation of William Henry Dawes, nephew of Sophie Dawes, the St. Helens smuggler's daughter who became a French Countess.

Even later in date was the park that was created around the newly built Weston Manor at Freshwater from 1881. This house was built for William Ward, grandson of George Ward, in a High Victorian Gothic style (Girouard 1971, 189). The surrounding park is shown on the 1909 Ordnance Survey 6 inch map.

On the other side of the Island, to the east of Ryde, the enlargement of Lord Calthorpe's house at Woodlands Vale by the noted architect Samuel Saunders Teulon in 1870-71 was accompanied by a corresponding enlargement of the grounds into a substantial park. A remarkable oriental garden at Woodlands Vale which may be contemporary with the 1870 remodelling of the house has survived in surprisingly good condition and is particularly worthy of conservation.

The Undercliff and The Landslip continued to attract wealthy settlers in the nineteenth century. Nature here had worked as a landscape gardener, creating natural terraces and fern covered boulders which appealed as strongly to the Victorian imagination as they had to earlier generations. The mild frost free climate and south facing slopes were added bonuses to the horticulturalist.

It was perhaps the dramatic backdrop of the Undercliff that led John Hamborough to erect the mock gothic Steephill Castle on the site of the recently demolished Steephill Cottage in the 1830's. The grounds were laid out by William Page, the Southampton landscape gardener who was later to remodel St. John's. Page's work at Steephill attracted praise from Joseph Paxton, one of the most noted professional gardeners of Victorian times. Paxton who was gardener to the Duke of Devonshire at Chatsworth, and later designed The Crystal Palace reputedly stated

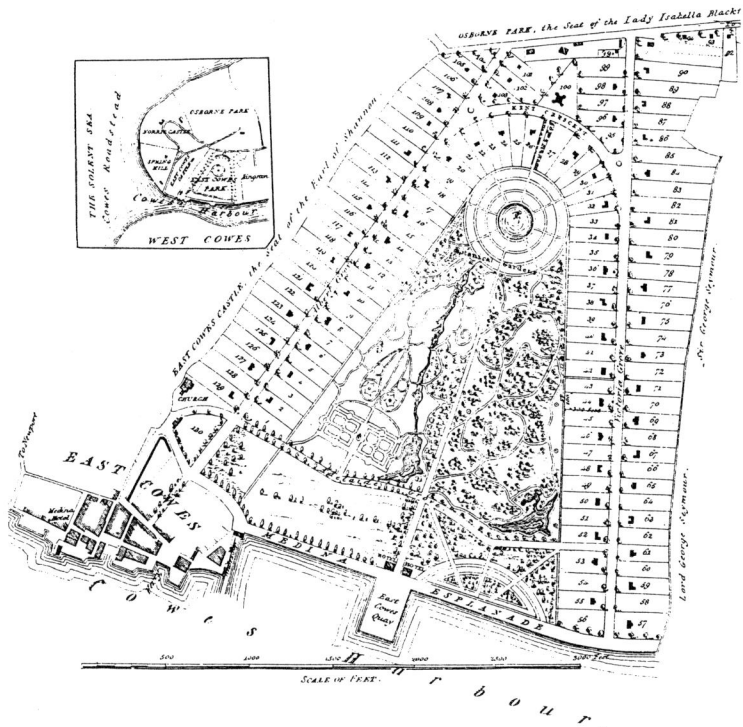

*Design for East Cowes Park and Botanical Gardens.
The layout of the Park shown on this plan was never completed.*

that "although he had travelled over the great part of Europe, and surveyed the most celebrated garden scenes, there was no place with which he was so much gratified as with the grounds of Steephill" (Cooke 1849). It should be said that the reporter of Paxton's remarks was sometimes given to hyperbole!

Another Undercliff estate improved in the nineteenth century was Old Park, near St. Lawrence. This had been a Worsley property in the eighteenth century and had various owners before coming into the possession of William Spindler in the later nineteenth century. Spindler had plans to develop Old Park and planted many trees on the estate, but his scheme for a seaside resort was abandoned on his death (Whitehead 1911). Amongst the garden features at Old Park are the remains of a water garden and a Gothic style summerhouse, but the date of these is not known.

Bonchurch, at the eastern end of the Undercliff, had been developed in early Victorian times. The romantic beauty of the village with its ornamental pond encouraged literary and artistic Victorians to visit or to settle here. Nearly all the new properties were large houses with substantial grounds. These included East Dene, the childhood home of the poet Swinburne, and Winterbourne, where Charles Dickens stayed in 1849. At Pulpit Rock, a property immediately below St. Boniface Down, the gardens seem to have been a curious mixture of the formal and the naturalistic, incorporating "parterres of fragrant flowers, ... winding paths along the terrace slopes ... sequestered alcoves, rocky grots and shady groves ..." (Cooke 1849). Just above the nineteenth century church of St. Boniface is the entrance to Cliff Dene, the home until 1951 of H. de Vere Stacpoole the writer, who described it as "this old Victorian wilderness of a garden" (Stacpoole 1937). This garden, now renamed *Yaffles*, has recently been restored (Wolfenden 1982).

Westfield at Ryde had been the villa of Earl Spencer in the early nineteenth century. It was a property which possessed typical Victorian gardens in an Italianate style. An engraving by E.A. Brooke (c 1850) shows a terraced garden with statues and garden temples.

There is little space here to mention public gardens or other large Victorian gardens associated with coastal and suburban development. Three interesting Victorian parks that were associated with contemporary housing estates must, however, be mentioned. Vernon Square in Ryde, surrounded by Victorian and Regency properties, was a communal garden for residents. The St. John's Park development, also in Ryde, was created in 1854 on land that had earlier been within the landscape park of St. John's. Unlike Vernon Square, St. John's Park was an irregular 'tear-drop' of land, entirely surrounded by houses whose owners were keyholders with access to the park. Amenities within the park included a band stand, two tennis courts, formal gardens and a variety of trees.

An altogether more ambitious project was East Cowes Park. An undated prospectus in the Isle of Wight County Record Office (c 1840's) shows the design for an estate of villas set around a central botanical garden. The area of the planned development was about 142 acres, and in 1859 it was stated that "about twenty handsome villas have been erected" (White 1859). Shortly afterwards the sad demise of the project was noted (Davenport Adams 1862) and it was felt that "the enterprising builder relied too heavily on the attractions of its proximity to Osborne". However a plan in the Isle of Wight County Record Office, dated 1874, shows that the botanical garden was actually created, although it was soon erased by ordinary residential development.

Twentieth Century Gardens

We are fortunate to have on the Island today a successful and thriving Botanic Garden, created in the grounds of the Royal National Hospital after the closure of this institution in the 1960's. The Ventnor Botanic Garden is one of the major twentieth century gardens created on the Isle of Wight, its interest being enhanced by the large old trees inherited from the hospital garden which was laid out from 1868 onwards (Laidlaw 1968).

A new garden on a far older site is at Mottistone Manor where the sixteenth century manor house lies in a sheltered combe which forms a superb setting for the modern garden. Several notable gardens of today, including Cedar Lodge (near Ryde), Little Brook and Tyne Hall (Bembridge), occupy old sites. These are among the Isle of Wight Gardens described by Allen Paterson (1978), some of which open annually under the National Gardens Scheme. Many of them can be described as 'plantsman's gardens' where much of the interest is provided by the unusual and exotic species which thrive in the mild Island climate. New private gardens have been created on a smaller scale in recent years in at least two Island villages and it is hoped that these will survive into the twenty-first century together with many of the historic parks and gardens described above.

PARKS AND GARDENS TODAY AND IN THE FUTURE

It can be seen from the large-scale Ordnance Surveys of 1866, 1898 and 1909 that an extremely large area of the Isle of Wight was occupied by private ornamental parks and gardens in the late nineteenth and early twentieth centuries. In the present century it has become increasingly difficult to maintain these grounds and their associated large houses. In and around the towns there has been a need for land to accommodate new residential development, particularly since the Second World War.

Two major historic houses, Steephill Castle and East Cowes Castle, were totally demolished in the 1960's and houses were built in the grounds. Other large houses survive, sometimes being divided into flats or used as offices, but the grounds have often been partially or completely developed, as at Brook House, Northwood Park, St. John's, Westfield (Ryde) and Westhill (Freshwater). Quite a large number of sites have been used for holiday camps or caravan sites, including Norton Lodge, Puckpool, St. Clare and Westcliff (Niton). The low-density development usual in holiday accommodation of this type has resulted in the survival of old trees and other garden features at some properties, although at other sites little of interest has survived. At Fairlee, part of the former landscape park is now an arboretum in the care of Medina Borough Council. Medina High School has been built on the site of the eighteenth century house.

The rural landscape parks, in their heyday, had a secondary agricultural use in addition to their ornamental function, for they were generally grazed by cattle and sheep. In the latter part of the twentieth century agricultural use has become far more intensive and in many cases the land use has changed from pastoral to arable farming. Frequently the farmed area of former parkland is in different ownership from that of the associated house. Nevertheless, many parkland trees of great landscape value have been preserved within areas that have reverted to agriculture, and ornamental trees also survive on public roads and private tracks which were formerly within the boundaries of large estates. Many of these surviving trees are now over-mature and require replanting. Examples of landscape parks which have now been partially returned to agriculture but which retain features of great value include Nunwell, Swainston and Westover.

At Appuldurcombe, the grandest eighteenth century landscape park on the Island, agricultural development has, sadly, almost completely destroyed the outer park. The inner park, however, is carefully preserved under the guardianship of English Heritage along with the shell of Appuldurcombe House which itself became derelict earlier this century.

The park at Osborne is exceptionally well preserved. Much of the parkland is in the care of English Heritage although other areas are used for agriculture, forestry and as a golf course.

Nearby, the parkland around Norris Castle is also well preserved, mainly as pasture.

In some instances traces of a former park or garden survive almost 'accidentally'. At Fernhill, to the west of Wootton Creek, some interesting features remain, although the house burnt down in 1938 and the grounds are now divided into a residential caravan site, pasture and a holiday camp. At Knighton the walled garden of possible seventeenth century origin remains undeveloped, although it is heavily overgrown with trees. The Victorian St. John's Park at Ryde is overgrown and semi-derelict although a number of trees survive and are protected by Tree Preservation Orders.

Statutory protection does not necessarily ensure the preservation of architectural features. The eighteenth century Grecian temple at Swainston is a listed building but fell into serious disrepair, although the facade has now been restored by the new owner. Ultimately legal protection will only be successful in preserving our surviving heritage of historic parks and gardens if it is complemented by a public awareness of their existence and their value.

The post-war decay of parks and gardens on the Island mirrored the situation nationally, except that many mainland parks were also damaged by motorway construction. Bodfan Gruffydd's publication *Protecting Historic Landscapes* which appeared in 1977 first drew public attention to the plight of historic parks and gardens. Official awareness increased gradually, especially following the creation of the Garden History Society in 1965 and the Centre for the Conservation of Historic Parks and Gardens, based at the University of York, in 1982.

The identification of those sites which are of substantial historic value is an important first step towards the conservation of parks and gardens. The National Heritage Act of 1983 stipulated that English Heritage should compile a Register of Parks and Gardens of special historic interest in England. The Register is now complete and has identified and described some 1200 nationally important historic parks and gardens throughout the country. Inclusion in the Register brings with it no statutory controls and restrictions. Its value lies in the dissemination of information, so that owners, local authorities and developers are made aware of the importance of this facet of our heritage.

The Register includes only six sites on the Isle of Wight. These are Appuldurcombe, Norris Castle, Nunwell, Osborne, Swainston and Westover (English Heritage 1987). Nationally, the Register places most emphasis on landscape parks, and on the Isle of Wight it ignores the picturesque gardens of the Undercliff and nineteenth century gardens such as that at Woodlands Vale. Information for the Register was drawn largely from printed sources, and counties where extensive field survey had previously been carried out and published are better represented in the Register. Only two Isle of Wight landscape parks, Appuldurcombe (Banks and Tandy 1980) and Osborne (Phibbs *et al* 1983), have been subjected to detailed survey. Potential sites of interest on the Island were identified in a survey carried out for the Island Planning Unit in 1987 but relatively few of these sites have yet been inspected on the ground (Basford 1987). There is no doubt that further field survey would identify more sites meriting inclusion in the Register.

To conserve parks and gardens of historic interest it is not enough simply to protect them from development and changes in land use. Gardens are living organisms; they rapidly decay if they are not adequately nurtured. They also present a paradox, in that they celebrate a human partnership with nature and yet there must be a constant struggle against nature to preserve the essential outline and design of the garden. Apart from the problem of maintenance there is also a need, where possible, to restore gardens that have fallen into decay. It is also desirable to educate and inform the public about the value of historic gardens. To fulfil these aims many counties have now established garden trusts. The Hampshire Gardens Trust has been operating for several years and has carried out numerous works of conservation and restoration within the County.

In 1989 a Gardens Trust was established on the Isle of Wight. This body will work in close partnership with the Isle of Wight Buildings Preservation Trust to encourage the conservation of the Island's historic buildings and their grounds, whether large or small. One important priority of the Gardens Trust is to carry out detailed field survey and recording of parks and gardens in order to identify features of historic interest which require conservation.

Financial assistance or practical help may be available from various national and local bodies to assist in the conservation of historic parks and gardens. Local owners are advised to contact the Island Planning Unit if they feel that they might qualify for grant aid. Practical help with tree planting can sometimes be provided by the Island's Countryside Management Service and help may also be available from the local branch of the British Trust for Conservation Volunteers.

'The Temple', Swainston, in decay, 1985. The portico of this listed building has now been restored.

It is heartening to realise that derelict gardens can be rescued and restored. The Victorian garden at Vernon Square in Ryde had become totally neglected in recent years and was, in fact, an eyesore. However, in 1986 the Vernon Square Preservation Society was formed following residents' concern over the condition of the site. The Society managed to purchase the site with the aid of a substantial donation and loan from descendants of the Langdon family who used to live in the Square. In 1988 workers employed by the County Council on a Community Programme project funded by the Government's Manpower Services Commission started to clear and restore the area. Grants were given to the project by the Isle of Wight Buildings Preservation Trust, by Medina Borough Council and by various local businesses. Historic features including a well from the Regency period, path networks, brickwork, a pergola and steps have been reinstated. New trees, shrubs and seats have been provided, and the Square has been re-enclosed with metal railings, replacing those that had been taken away in the War. The project is planned for completion in June 1989.

Many private owners on the Isle of Wight successfully maintain large grounds in the face of considerable difficulties while others are maintained by public bodies. Osborne and the inner park at Appuldurcombe are carefully conserved by English Heritage. The National Trust is the owner of one important Island garden – at Mottistone Manor – and the two Borough Councils of Medina and South Wight own a number of parks and gardens of historic and contemporary interest. Medina Borough Council is responsible for Northwood Park, Appley and Puckpool, whilst the most important site in the care of South Wight Borough Council is Ventnor Botanic Garden. Here a splendid new temperate house was erected in 1986 but the Garden suffered terribly in the 'Great Storm' of October 1987 as did Osborne and, indeed, most Island gardens. Happily much restoration work has already taken place.

The Isle of Wight County Council and the two borough councils bear a special responsibility for historic parks and gardens which are a valuable part of the Island's heritage. With the growth of the leisure industry those parks and gardens which are open to the public will be of increasing importance to tourism, although the conflicting demands of visitor access and conservation must be carefully balanced. Any plans for remodelling sites in the care of the local authorities must respect their historic origins.

The Vernon Square Project is a pioneering effort on the Isle of Wight and shows what can be achieved by a combination of local concern, voluntary help and contributions from national and local government. We must hope that more garden restoration projects will soon be under way on the Isle of Wight together with the equally important recording and educational work that will be necessary to conserve our heritage of historic parks and gardens. In the last analysis, however, we are dependent on the practical and dedicated gardeners who labour long hours in their gardens to create an annual display of beauty and a garden heritage which, with careful tending, will survive for the enjoyment of future generations.

GAZETTEER OF ISLE OF WIGHT LANDSCAPE PARKS AND GARDENS PRE-DATING 1825

This gazetteer lists ninety eight Isle of Wight landscape parks and gardens which were of some importance in the second half of the eighteenth century and the first quarter of the nineteenth century. It does not show medieval or early formal gardens unless these continued to be of significance in the later eighteenth century.

The gazetteer does not list the large number of private parks and gardens created in the Victorian period. Over 250 such parks and gardens are shaded on the 1866 six inch Ordnance survey map of the Isle of Wight, in addition to the ninety eight sites listed here. Many of these Victorian gardens were attached to suburban villas around the developing Island towns. No fieldwork has yet been carried out to assess the historical significance or condition of these later gardens.

Landscape parks and gardens pre-dating 1825 are listed in the gazetteer if they are shown on one or more of the following four maps *A Topographical Map of the Isle of Wight*, John Andrews 1769 (1st edition). *Map of the Isle of Wight* published by Sir Richard Worsley 1781 in his *History of the Isle of Wight. A Military, Marine and Topographical Survey of the Isle of Wight*, James Clarke 1812. *A New Map of the Isle of Wight* published by George Brannon 1824 in *Vectis Scenery*. All four maps identify "Noblemen's and Gentlemen's Seats" and/or show shaded areas of parkland or garden. Clarke depicts the major landscape parks by means of conventionalised park pales. Andrews prints the owner's name beside each park or garden.

A few of the gardens marked on the maps were not pleasure grounds although they have been included in the gazetteer for the sake of completeness. The House of Industry Garden at Parkhurst, for instance, was obviously a productive rather than ornamental garden.

The gazetteer entries are arranged by nineteenth century ecclesiastical parishes as shown on the 1866 1st edition Ordnance Survey six inch maps. It has not been possible to use civil parishes as names and boundaries have altered several times since the late nineteenth century. All National Grid References given in the gazetteer entry should carry the prefix SZ. National Grid Reference is abbreviated to N.G.R.

GAZETTEER

PARISH	SITE	N.G.R. S.Z.	ANDREWS 1769	WORSLEY 1781	CLARKE 1812	BRANNON 1824
ARRETON						
	Arreton Rectory	534866				●
	Champion	501850	●		●	
	East Standen	525871			●	
	Fernhill	540915			●	●
	Pidford	504857	●	●	●	●
	Standen	507871	●	●	●	●
	Staplers	515893	●	●		
	Stickworth	540853			●	●
BINSTEAD						
	Binstead Parsonage	575928				●
	Binstead House	576929			●	●
	Kite Hill	549919				●
	Quarr Abbey (Farm)	566926			●	
BONCHURCH						
	St. Boniface Cottage	570780			●	●
BRADING						
	Heath Barracks	592840			●	
	Landguard Manor	580824	●			
	Nunwell	596874	●	●	●	●
	Sandham Cottage	599842		●		
BROOK						
	Brook House	392842	●	●		
CALBOURNE						
	Locks	444909			●	
	Swainston	441877	●	●	●	●
	Westover	423863	●	●		●
CARISBROOKE						
	Alvington	475886	●	●		
	House of Industry	495902			●	

66

PARISH	SITE	N.G.R. S.Z.	ANDREWS 1769	WORSLEY 1781	CLARKE 1812	BRANNON 1824
CHALE						
	Sandrock Cottage	489762				•
FRESHWATER						
	Afton Park	349869	•	•	•	•
	Farringford Park	337861				•
	Freshwater Farm	349881				•
	Grange, Compton	379842			•	
	Norton Lodge	345897				•
	Westhill	341898				•
GATCOMBE						
	Gatcombe Park	493850	•	•	•	•
	Gatcombe Rectory	484852				•
	Little Gatcombe	484852	•	•		
	Sheat	494845	•	•		
GODSHILL						
	Appuldurcombe	543801	•	•	•	•
	Fairfield	508797			•	
	The Hermitage	498788				•
	Rookley Cottage	507840				•
	Steephill Cottage	554773	•	•	•	•
	Stenbury	525790	•			
NEWCHURCH						
	Buckingham Villa	590928				•
	Knighton Manor	566869	•	•	•	
	Earl Spencer's Marine Villa	588929			•	•
	Ryde House	582929			•	•
	Wackland	553849				•
	Westmont	589925				•

GAZETTEER

PARISH	SITE	N.G.R. S.Z.	ANDREWS 1769	WORSLEY 1781	CLARKE 1812	BRANNON 1824
NITON						
	Beauchamp	511761				●
	Niton Parsonage	508767			●	
	Orchard	513761				●
	Puckaster Cottage	509759				●
	Westcliff	504761				●
NORTHWOOD						
	Cliff, Gurnard	470951			●	
	Egypt House	484965			●	●
	Lord Grantham's Marine Villa	492966				●
	Hillis	469933			●	
	Medham	495936			●	●
	Moorhouse	491955				●
	Northwood Park	493963				●
	Westhill House	496957				●
PARKHURST						
	Lodge	471915			●	
ST. HELENS						
	Appley	603925	●	●	●	●
	Fairy Hill	624910			●	●
	The Priory	632903	●	●	●	●
	Puckpool House	613921				●
	St. Clare	611921				●
	St. Johns House	603920			●	●
	Seafield House	626917			●	
	Seagrove	630911				●
ST. LAWRENCE						
	St. Lawrence Cottage (Sea Cottage)	541767			●	●

GAZETTEER

PARISH	SITE	N.G.R. S.Z.	ANDREWS 1769	WORSLEY 1781	CLARKE 1812	BRANNON 1824
SHALFLEET						
	Bouldnor	373898			●	
	Churchills	398868			●	
	Cranmore	390899			●	
	Hamstead	399913			●	
	Ningwood House	402888			●	●
SHANKLIN						
	Shanklin Manor	577807	●	●		●
SHORWELL						
	Billingham	486819	●	●		●
	North Court	456833	●	●	●	●
	Woolverton	453824	●	●		
	Yafford	451817	●	●	●	●
THORLEY						
	Thorley	367891	●	●	●	
WHIPPINGHAM						
	Barton Manor	520944	●	●		
	Belle Croft	511894				●
	East Cowes Castle	509955				●
	Elm Cottage	509958				●
	Fairlee House	507904	●	●	●	●
	New Fairlee	515898	●			
	Millfield	510958				●
	Norris Castle	516858				●
	Osborne	516948	●	●	●	●
	Padmore	515933	●	●		●
	St. Thomas	506959				●
	Shide Lodge	504880				●
	Slatwoods	503959				●
	Springhill	510960				●
WHITWELL						
	Mirables	521760			●	●
WOOTTON						
	Wootton Lodge	541921				●
YARMOUTH						
	The Mount	358897			●	●
YAVERLAND						
	Yaverland Parsonage	615855				●

PARKS AND GARDENS OPEN TO THE PUBLIC

Many of the places described or illustrated in the text are private property and are **not** open to the public.

A list of *Places of Interest* is available from any of the Tourist Information Centres of Medina and South Wight Borough Councils. Sandown and Shanklin Tourist Information Centres are open all the year. The following parks and gardens are included in the published list for 1989. Admission charges and times of opening are given in the list.

Appuldurcombe House, Wroxall, near Ventnor
Barton Manor Vineyard and Gardens, Whippingham
Carisbrooke Castle, Privy Garden
Morton Manor, House, Gardens and Vineyard, Brading
Mottistone Manor Gardens
Nunwell House and Gardens, Brading
Osborne House. Limited access to grounds and terraces

Medina Borough Council maintains the following grounds:

Appley Park, Ryde
Arboretum, Fairlee Road, Newport
Litten Park, Newport
Northwood Park, Cowes
Puckpool Park, Ryde
St. Thomas' Rest Garden, Ryde

South Wight Borough Council is responsible for the following grounds:

Battery Gardens, Sandown
Lake Cliff Gardens
Rylstone Gardens, Shanklin
Sandham Grounds, Sandown
Tower Gardens, Shanklin
Ventnor Botanic Gardens and Temperate House
Ventnor Park

Certain privately owned gardens are opened for one afternoon each year under the National Gardens Scheme. A list of gardens open under this scheme is issued annually and can be obtained from any tourist information centre or public library.

REFERENCES

ANDREWS, J.:(1769)
A Topographical Map of the Isle of Wight in Hampshire, London

ANTHONY, J.:(1985)
Discovering Period Gardens, 2 edn, Aylesbury

APPULDURCOMBE :(1571)
Rental for the Manor of Appuldurcombe, Isle of Wight County Record Office, JER/WA/32/11

BAKER, T.:(1799)
Companion in a tour round Southampton, Southampton

BAMFORD, F. ed.:(1936)
A Royalist's Notebook: The Commonplace Book of Sir John Oglander, London

BANKS, E.:(1987)
A Review of the Park at Appuldurcombe, Isle of Wight, report commissioned by the I.W. Joint Planning and Technical Unit, Land Use Consultants, London

BANKS, E., SWANWICK, C. and NELSON, P.:(1983)
A Study of Gardens and Designed Landscapes in Scotland, Countryside Commission for Scotland

BANKS, E. and TANDY, C.R.V.:(1980)
The Proposals for the Restoration of the Landscape at Appuldurcombe House, report commissioned by the Department of the Environment, Land Use Consultants, London

BARBER, T.:(1834)
Picturesque illustrations of the Isle of Wight, London

BARRINGTON, T.:(1631)
A note of our woods and lands in Carisbrooke parke, Ms, April 1631, Isle of Wight County Record Office, Swainston Papers No. 1174

BASFORD, H.V.:(1980)
The Vectis Report. A Survey of Isle of Wight Archaeology, Isle of Wight County Council, Newport

BASFORD, H.V.:(1987)
Isle of Wight Historic Parks & Gardens, unpublished report prepared for the Island Planning Unit

REFERENCES

BATEY, M.:(1987)
"The New Forest and the Picturesque", *in* Hedley, G. and Rance, A. (ed): *Pleasure Grounds. The Gardens & Landscapes of Hampshire*, Horndean

BEVIS, J.H., KETTEL, R.E and SHEPARD, B.:(1978)
Flora of the Isle of Wight, Newport

BILIKOWSKI, K.:(1983)
Hampshire's Countryside Heritage. 5: Historic Parks and Gardens, Hampshire County Council, Winchester

BILIKOWSKI, K.:(1986)
Unpublished notes concerning some Isle of Wight parks and gardens. Deposited at the Isle of Wight Joint Planning Technical Unit.

BILIKOWSKI, K.:(1987)
"Formal Gardens in Hampshire", *in* Hedley, G. and Rance, A. (ed): *Pleasure Grounds. The Gardens & Landscapes of Hampshire*, Horndean

BISHOP LOVETT SCHOOL HISTORY CLUB :(1979)
The Origin of a School Building. Two Hundred Years at St. Johns House, Ryde

BODFAN GRUFFYDD, J.St.:(1977)
Protecting Historic Landscape, The Landscape Institute

BOYNTON, L.O.J.:(1967)
Appuldurcombe House, H.M.S.O., London

BRANNON, G.:(1824)
Vectis Scenery, Wootton

BRANNON, G.:(1837)
The Pleasure Visitor's Companion, 5 edn, Wootton

BRITTON, J. AND BRAYLEY, E.W.:(1804)
A Topographical and Historical Description of the County of Hampshire, and Isle of Wight, London

BROOKE, E.A.:(C 1850)
View in the Gardens of Westfield House, Isle of Wight. The seat of Sir Augustus Clifford, Bart., engraving.

C.P.R. :(1350)
Calendar of the Patent Rolls 1350, **4**, 288, Public Record Office, London

CAMDEN, W.:(1637)
Britannia, 273, London

CANTOR, L.M. and WILSON, J.D.:(1961–1969)
"The Medieval Deer-Parks of Dorset", *Proc. Dorset Nat. Hist. & Archaeol. Soc.*, **83–91**

CARTER, G., GOODE, P. and LAURIE, K.:(1982)
Humphry Repton Landscape Gardener 1752–1818, Sainsbury Centre for Visual Arts, Norwich

REFERENCES

CAWS, S. and BRINTON, R.E.:(1983)
Cowes and East Cowes Past and Present, Isle of Wight County Council, Newport

CHARLTON, J.:(1986)
Osborne House, English Heritage, London

COOKE, W.:(1808)
A New Picture of the Isle of Wight, London

COOKE, W.B.:(1849)
Bonchurch, Shanklin & the Undercliff, London

CUNLIFFE, B.:(1971)
Fishbourne. A Roman Palace and its Garden, London

DAVENPORT ADAMS, W.H.:(1862)
Nelson's Handbook to the Isle of Wight, London

DONNE, S.:(1773)
Survey of the Nunwell Estate, Isle of Wight County Record Office OG/PP/13

ENGLEFIELD, SIR H.C.:(1816)
A Description of the Principal Picturesque Beauties, Antiquities and Geological Phenomena of the Isle of Wight, London

ENGLISH HERITAGE:(1987)
Register of Parks & Gardens of Special Historic Interest in England. Part 23. Isle of Wight, Historic Buildings and Monuments Commission for England, London

FOWLER, P.:(1983)
Farms in England, prehistoric to present, 33, Royal Commission on Historical Monuments England, London

FLEMING, L. and GORE, A.:(1979)
The English Garden, London

GILPIN, W.:(1798)
Observations on the Western Parts of England relative chiefly to Picturesque Beauty to which are added a few remarks on the Picturesque Beauties of the Isle of Wight, London

GIROUARD, M.:(1971)
The Victorian Country House, Oxford

HOCKEY, S.F.:(1970)
Quarr Abbey and Its Lands 1132–1631, Leicester

HOCKEY, S.F.:(1981)
The Cartulary of Carisbrooke Priory, Newport

HOCKEY, S.F.:(1982)
Insula Vecta, Chichester

HUTCHINGS, R.J. and HINTON, B. eds:(1986)
The Farringford Journal of Emily Tennyson 1853–1864, Newport

REFERENCES

JASHEMSKI, W.F.:(1979)
The Gardens of Pompeii, Herculaneum and the Villas Destroyed by Vesuvius, New York

JONES, J.D.:(1978)
The Isle of Wight 1588–1642, unpublished Ph.D. thesis, University of Southampton

JONES J. AND JONES J.:(1987)
The Isle of Wight. An Illustrated History, Wimborne

KITCHIN, T.:(1764)
A New Map of The Isle of Wight

KÖKERITZ, H.:(1940)
The Place-Names of the Isle of Wight, Uppsala

LAIDLAW, E.F.:(1968)
"The Gardens of the Royal National Hospital", *Proc. I.W. Nat. Hist. & Archaeol. Soc.*, **6**, 195–204

LANDSBERG, S.:(n.d.)
The Tudor Garden, Tudor House, Bugle Street, Southampton, Southampton Museums

LANDSBERG, S.:(1987)
"The Re-creation of a Medieval and a 16th. century Garden in Hampshire": *in* Hedley, G. and Rance, A. (ed) 1987, *Pleasure Grounds. The Gardens & Landscapes of Hampshire*, Horndean

MACLEAN, T.:(1981)
Medieval Gardens, London

NOYES, A.:(1939)
Orchard's Bay, London

OGLANDER :(1748)
A Plan of Nunwell House and Gardens, Together with the Offices, Farmyard, Barns, Stabling, and the Lands Adjacent, map in possession of Mrs. Oglander

OGLANDER Mss.
Ms. Commonplace book of Sir John Oglander, Isle of Wight County Record Office OG/AA/14

PAGE, W. ed.:(1912)
A History of Hampshire and the Isle of Wight, **5**, The Victoria History of the Counties of England, London

PATERSON, A.:(1978)
The Gardens of Britain 2: Dorset, Hampshire & the Isle of Wight, London

PHIBBS, J.L. *et al*:(1983)
Royal Parks Historic Survey: Osborne, Isle of Wight, Survey commissioned by the Directorate of Ancient Monuments and Historic Buildings, Department of the Environment, London

PINHORN, M.:(1987)
"Isle of Wight Weekend", *Garden History Society Newsletter*, **20**, 5

PRICE, J.E. and PRICE, F.G.H.:(1881)
Remains of Roman Buildings at Morton near Brading, London

POPE, C.:(1981)
"Non-flowering Plants – Notes for 1981: Lichens", *Proc. I.W. Nat. Hist. & Archaeol. Soc.*, **7** (1983), 393

RACKHAM, O.:(1986)
The History of the Countryside, London

ROBERTS, E.:(1988)
"The Bishop of Winchester's Deer Parks in Hampshire, 1200–1400", *Proc. Hants. Field Club*, **44**, 67–86

SEALE, A. ED.:(1983)
Barrington Family Letters 1628–1637, Royal Historical Society, Camden Fourth Series, **28**

SHIRLEY, E.P.:(1867)
Some Account of English Deer Parks: with notes on the management of deer, John Murray

SPENCER, J., COX, J. and CHATTERS, C.:(1987)
Isle of Wight Inventory of Ancient Woodlands, Nature Conservancy Council, Peterborough

STACPOOLE, H. de VERE :(1937)
In a Bonchurch Garden, London

STONE, P.G.:(1891)
The Architectural Antiquities of the Isle of Wight, London

STROUD, D.:(1950)
Capability Brown, Country Life, London

STROUD, D.:(1962)
Humphry Repton, Country Life, London

SUMMERSON, J.:(1935)
John Nash, London

TAYLOR, C.:(1983)
The Archaeology of Gardens, Aylesbury

TEMPLE, N.:(1987)
"Pages from an architect's notebook: John Nash; some minor buildings in the Isle of Wight Part 1.", *Proc. I.W. Nat. Hist. & Archaeol. Soc.*, **8**, (2)

TENNYSON, C.:(1976)
Farringford – Home of Alfred Lord Tennyson, The Tennyson Society, Lincoln

THACKER, C.:(1979)
The History of Gardens, London

TOMALIN, D.J.:(1987)
Roman Wight – A Guide Catalogue, Isle of Wight County Council, Newport

REFERENCES

TOMKINS C.:(1796)
Tour to the Isle of Wight, vol 2, London

TURNER, T.:(1986)
English Garden Design, Antique Collector's Club

WHITE, W.:(1859)
History, Gazetteer & Directory of Hampshire & the Isle of Wight, Sheffield and London

WHITEHEAD, J.L.:(1911)
The Undercliff of the Isle of Wight, Ventnor

WILLIAMSON, T. and BELLAMY, L.:(1987)
Property and Landscape, chapters 7 and 8, London

WILSON, J.D.:(1970–1978)
"The Medieval Deer-Parks of Dorset, X–XVII", *Proc. Dorset Nat. Hist. & Archaeol. Soc.*, **92–100**

WINTER, C.W.R.:(1984)
The Manor Houses of The Isle of Wight, Wimborne

WOLFENDEN. J.:(1982)
The Glory of the Garden & The Cycle of the Year, Bonchurch

WORSLEY ACCTS.
Worsley Account Books, Isle of Wight County Record Office, JER/WA/33/6

WORSLEY, SIR R.:(1781)
History of the Isle of Wight, London.

INDEX

Aerial photography 45
Afton 48
Albert, Prince 11, 46, 48, 56
Alpine bridge, Northcourt 48
Alvington 48
Amherst, Colonel William 53
Amice, Countess of Devon 16
Ancient woodland 17
Annuals 57
Appley, Ryde 48, 64
Appuldurcombe 16, 23, 30, 32, 35, 49, 50, 61, 62, 64
   Down 36, 41
   House 23, 36, 41, 61
   Park 9–11, 35, 42
   Wood 36, 42
Arboretum 42, 61
Arbour 22
Arbour garden 20
Arbutus 49
Archways 52
Arts and Crafts Movement 30
Avenues 26, 29, 30, 35, 42
Avington Forest 13
Azaleas 54

Balustrades 42, 57
Band stand, St. John's Park 60
Baroque 32
Barrington
   Family 30
   Sir Thomas 14
Barton Manor 22, 25, 48, 56
Battery 50
Bedding out 57
Beech 54
Bellevue House, Cowes 54
Betty Haunt Lane 13, 14
Billingham Manor 23, 25, 48
Binstead Parsonage 52
Bisset, George 23
Bitterne, Hants 16
Blachford
   Lady Isabella 56
   Robert Pope 46, 48, 56, 57
Blomfield, Reginald 30
Bonchurch 50, 59
Botanic Garden
   East Cowes 60
   Ventnor 60
Boundary belt 56
Bowcombe Valley 20
Bowling greens 23, 25, 26, 28
Brading Roman Villa 19
Bridgeman, Charles 29
Brook House 48, 58, 61
Brown, 'Capability' 29, 30, 32, 36, 41, 49, 56
Buckingham, Duke of 52
Budbridge Manor 25
Buildings Preservation Trust 63, 64
Bull, Richard 48
Burgage plots 19

Calbourne Heathfield 16
Calthorpe, Lord 58
Canals 29
'Capability' Brown
   see Brown
Caravan sites 61, 62
Carisbrooke Castle 14, 20
Carriage drive 45, 56
Cartulary, Carisbrooke Priory 20
Cedar Lodge, Ryde 60
Chapel of St. Nicholas
   Carisbrooke 22
Chase 13, 14, 17, 28
Chatsworth, Derbys 58
Chessell Park 16
Chilton Candover, Hants 35
Chinoiserie 30, 57
Cleveland Wood 36
Cliff Dene, Bonchurch 60
Commonplace Book, Sir J. Oglander's 25
Coneys 16
Conservation Volunteers
   British Trust for 63
Conservatory 48
Cook's Castle 10, 41
Cottage garden 30
Cottage ornée 52
Cottages ornées 11, 49–52
Countryside Management Service 63
Cubitt, Thomas 56
Cummin 20

Dairy, Northcourt 48
Dawes
   Sophie 58
   William Henry 58
De Estur family 16
De Parco family 17
De Redvers family 14
Debourne Lodge 54
Deer 16, 36, 46
Deer parks 9, 11, 13, 36
Dell, The, Northcourt 48
Developers 62
Devil's Bridge, Steephill 50
Dickens, Charles 59
Dingley, John 23
Disemparkment 14
Domesday Book 13
Doric lodge, Northwood Park 54
Dovecote 20
Dovehouse 23, 26
Druids's Temple, Fernhill 49

Earthworks 9, 25, 45
East Cowes Castle 54, 61
East Cowes Park 60
East Dene, Bonchurch 59
East Nunwell 26
Edward I, King 22
Edward VII, King 48
Elm 54
Emparkment 9, 13, 16, 36

Englefield, Sir Henry 23, 42
English Baroque 32
English Forest Style 29, 30
English Heritage 61, 62, 64
Estate cottages 10
Exotics 29, 30, 49, 52, 57, 60
Expansion of parkland 9, 36, 41
Eye-catcher 41

Fairlee 48, 61
Fairy Hill, St. Helen's 52, 54
Fake ruins 41
Fallow deer 13
Farringford 57, 58
Fatting Park, Shorwell 16
Fattingpark, Wootton 17
Fermes ornées 54
Fernery, Farringford 58
Fernhill 49, 62
Fishbourne Roman Palace 18, 25
Fishponds, Nunwell 26
Floral bedding 30, 57
Follies 10, 32, 54
Forecourts 23, 56
Forest 14
Forests 13
Formal gardens 18, 20, 26, 28–30, 32, 35, 36, 42, 60
Formal woodland 29, 30
Fortibus, Isabella de 20
Fountains 57
Free warren 16
Freemantle Close 36
Freemantle Gate 10, 36, 41
Freshwater Parish 17, 58
Frogmore, Berks 57

Garden History Society 62
Garden walls 10, 32
Gardenesque Style 29
Gardens Trusts 63
Gassiot, John Peter 54
Gatcombe
   Manor 22, 42
   Mill 45
   Park 9, 11, 45, 46
Gate piers, Knighton 23
Gates 41, 42
Gateway, Sea Cottage 50
Gazebo 23
Geometric gardens 20
Gillingham, Dorset 14
Gilpin, William 29, 49
Godshill Park 35
Gordon, Gen. Sir W. 52
Gothic folly 54
Gothic shrine 51
Gotten Manor 22
Great Avenue, Osborne 56
Great Park
   Shorwell 16
   Watchingwell 11
Grecian temple, Swainston 10, 32, 62

77

Green Park, Undercliff 16
Greenhouses 29, 50, 57
Grotto 54
Grüner, Ludwig 56
Ha-ha 29, 32, 41, 42, 46, 56, 58
Hamborough, John 58
Hampshire Gardens Trust 63
Hampton Court 50
Haseley Manor 25
Henry III, King 16
Herb gardens 19, 22
Herbaceous borders 30
Herbary 22
Herculaneum 25
Hermitage, Steephill 50
Hill Farm, Gatcombe 45
Holiday camps 61, 62
Holmes, Leonard Troughear 45
Hop gardens 26
Hunting ground 13, 14, 17
Hunting lodge 16

I.W. County Council 64
Ice houses 10
Isabella de Fortibus 20
Isle of Wight Joint Planning Unit 62, 63
Italianate Style 11, 29, 56, 57, 60

Jacobean garden, Northcourt 25
James, John 35
Jekyll, Gertrude 30
Jones, Inigo 50

Kent, William 29
King James Grammar School, Newport 20
King's Forest 14
King's Park 13
Kingston Manor 16, 25
Kitchen garden 36, 42, 46, 56, 57
Knight, Sir Richard Payne 29
Knighton Gorges 22, 23, 62
Knot garden 25, 26

Lady Wood, Swainston 32
Lake 23, 45
Landscape parks 9, 11, 30, 36, 41, 48
Landslip 58
Langdon family 64
Leasowes, Halesowen 54
Leigh, Sir John 25
Leisure industry 64
Lichens 16, 17
Lime, small-leaved 17
Limes 26
Lisle Combe 50, 51
Lisle family 14
Little Brook 60
Little Park
    Carisbrooke 17
    Shorwell 16
Local authorities 62
Lodges 10, 35, 42, 45, 49, 53, 54, 57, 58
London, George 32

Long Walk, Nunwell 42
Longleat, Wilts 32
Loudon, J.C. 30
Lower Fatting Park, Shorwell 16
Lutyens, Sir Edwin 30

Madonna Lily 19
Manor houses 22, 25
Marina, St. John's 53
Marine villas 11, 51, 52
Mary Gardens 19
Mausoleum 48
Medieval Gardens 19
Medina Borough 14
Medina Borough Council 61, 64
Medina High School 61
Memorial trees 57
Merdon, Hants 16
Merry Gardens 19
Merstone Manor 25
Metallic Hot House Manufactory 57
Meux family 16
Milton Abbas, Dorset 36
Mirables 52
Moated sites 22
Mock gothic 41
Model farm 48
Monasteries, dissolution 17
Monastic gardens 19
Montebourg, abbey of 17
Mosaiculture 30
Mottistone Manor 11, 60, 64
Mount 25, 48
Mount Ararat, Northcourt 48
Mulberry 28

Nash, John 42, 45, 54
National Gardens Scheme 60
National Heritage Act 62
National Trust 64
New College, Oxford 25
New Park, Watchingwell 14
Newport 19, 20
Newport Chantry 20
Newtown 19
Nodes Point 48
Norris Castle 41, 54, 56, 62
Norris farm 54
North Park Coppice, Freshwater 17
North Park Copse
    Calbourne 16
    Freshwater 17
North Park, Freshwater 17
Northcourt, Shorwell 25, 48
Northwood Park 10, 54, 56, 61, 64
Norton Lodge, Freshwater 57, 61
Noyes, Alfred 51
Nunwell 17, 20, 25, 28, 42, 61, 62

Obelisk 41
Oglander family 25
Oglander Glynn, John 42
Oglander, Robert 20

Oglander, Sir John 17, 25, 42
Old Park
    Undercliff 16, 59
    Watchingwell 14
Orchard, The, Niton 52
Orchards 20, 23, 26, 29, 42
Oriental garden 58
Osborne 11, 36, 46, 48, 56, 57, 60, 61, 62, 64
Owners 62

Padmore 48
Page, W.B. 54, 58
Park Farm, Brading 17
Park Hill, Shalfleet 16
Park Lane, Shorwell 16
Park pale 13, 14, 35
Park Place, Carisbrooke 17
Park place-names 17
Parkhurst Forest 13
Parterres 26, 29, 59
Partridges 26
Pavilion Wing, Osborne House 56
Pavilion, Sea Cottage 50
Paxton, Joseph 58
Pelham, Charles
    Lord Yarborough 42, 52
Pennethorne, James 56
Pergola 22, 64
Pheasants 26
Picturesque Movement 29, 32, 41, 49, 50
Pidford 48
Pigeon-house 26
Plant introduction 28
Plantations 53, 54
Plantsman's gardens 30, 60
Player family 52
Player, George 52
Pleasa(u)nce 23, 54
Pleasure gardens 18–20, 22, 32, 48
Pleasure grounds 11, 22, 30, 46, 48, 49, 52, 56
Pompeii 25
Ponds 20, 26, 32, 48, 59
Powlett, Thomas Orde
    Lord Bolton 49
Price, Sir Uvedale 29
Priory
    Appuldurcombe 17
    St. Cross, Newport 20
    St. Helen's 48
    St. Mary's, Carisbrooke 20
Priory Bay 48
Priory, The, St. Helen's 48
Privy garden, Carisbrooke Castle 22
Public gardens 60
Puckaster Cottage, Niton 51
Puckpool, Ryde 52, 61, 64
Pulpit Rock, Bonchurch 59
Pylewell, Hants 35

Quarr Abbey 19
Queen Eleanor's Garden, Winchester 22

Rabbits 16, 26

Raised walks 23, 25
Red Books of Humphry Repton 53, 54
Red deer 13
Register of Parks and Gardens 62
Repton, George 54
Repton, Humphry 29, 53, 54, 56
Rhododendrons 54
River Medina 45
Robinson, William 30
Rock gardens 54
Roe deer 13
Roman Gardens 18, 25
Roman villas 19
Romantic Movement 29, 49
Roses 19
Round House, Northwood Park 54
Royal estate, Osborne 48
Royal forests 13
Royal National Hospital, Ventnor 60
Royal Naval College, Osborne 57
Ryde House 52

Salisbury, Earls of 16, 22
Sandham Cottage 49
Sea Cottage, St. Lawrence 50, 51
Sea Grove, St. Helen's 52
Seely family 58
Serpentine drive, Appuldurcombe 41
Serpentine Style 29
Serpentine walks, Mirables 52
Seymour, Lord Henry 54
Shalfleet Manor 16
Shalfleet Park 16
Sheat Manor 23, 48
Shenstone, William 54
Shepard, Bill 49
Shorwell 16
Shrubberies 48, 49, 52, 54, 57
Shugborough, Staffs. 57
Simeon, Edward 53
Simeon, Sir John 54
Skating pond, Osborne 48
Soilmarks, Gatcombe 45
South Wight Borough 14
South Wight Borough Council 64
Specimen trees 57
Spencer, Earl 52, 60
Spindler, William 59
St. Boniface Cottage, Bonchurch 50
St. Clare, Ryde 52, 61
St. John's Park, Ryde 60, 62
St. John's, Ryde 10, 53, 54, 58, 60, 61
St. Laurence Park 14
St. Lawrence Cottage 51
St. Lawrence Well 51
St. Martin's Down 36, 41
St. Mary's Church, Cowes 54
St. Nicholas Parish 14
Stacpoole, H. de Vere 60
Standen 48
Stanley, Hans 50
Staplers 48

Statuary 57
Steephill Castle 58, 61
Steephill Cottage 50, 58
Stenbury Down 36
Stenbury Manor 22
Storm damage 56, 64
Summerhouses 23, 32, 48, 52, 58, 59
Sundial 22
Swainston 10, 14, 16, 22, 30, 32, 61, 62
Sweetwater Copse, Westover 45
Sweetwater Lodge, Westover 45
Swinburne, Algernon 59
Swiss cottage, Osborne 57
Switzer, Stephen 29

Temperate house, Ventnor 64
Temple of the Sun, Northcourt 48
Temple, The, Swainston 10, 32, 62
Temples 49, 50, 60
Tennis courts 23, 60
Tennyson
    Alfred Lord 58
    Emily 58
Terraces 23, 25, 28–30, 42, 48, 50, 51, 52, 56–58, 60
Teulon, Samuel Saunders 58
Thorley 17
Tofts 45
Toll-house, Northwood Park 54
Tourism 64
Tree planting 63
Tree Preservation Orders 62
Trenchard, Henry 54
Tudor and Jacobean Gardens 23
Tudor Garden, Southampton 25
Twentieth Century 60
Tyne Hall, Bembridge 60

Undercliff 14, 50, 51, 58, 59
Urns 57

Venison 13, 16
Ventnor Botanic Garden 60, 64
Vernon Square, Ryde 60, 64
Versailles 29
Victoria, Queen 11, 46, 48, 56
Victorian gardens 60, 64
Victorian parks 60
Vine, James 51
Vines 26
Vineyard 50
Vistas 48

Walled garden 23, 49, 52, 56, 62
Wallflower 20
Ward
    George 54, 58
    William 58
Warren 16, 26, 28, 42
Warren Hill, Kingston 16
Watch tower, St. Helen's 48
Watchingwell 13
Watchingwell Park 14, 17
Water features 29

Water garden 25, 48, 54, 59
Watts, William 36
Wellingtonia 58
West Nunwell 25
West Wight 57
Westcliff, Niton 61
Westfield, Ryde 60, 61
Westhill, Freshwater 57, 61
Weston Manor, Freshwater 58
Westover 10, 11, 45, 46, 49, 61, 62
Westover Copse 45
Westover Plantation 45
Weymouth, Viscount 32
Wheelbarrow Cottage, Westover 45
Whippingham 17
Whitecroft 45
Wild Garden 30
Wilderness 48, 58
Wilkes, John 49
Willy Wood, Swainston 32
Wilton Abbey, Wilts 13
Winchester College 48
Winchester, Bishops of 16, 19, 22
Winifred's Well, Swainston 32
Winterbourne, Bonchurch 59
Wood pasture 13
Woodland, ancient 17
Woodlands Vale, Ryde 58
Woolverton
    Shorwell 22
    Undercliff 16
Wootton 17, 49
Wootton Manor 14, 22
Wootton Park 14
Worsley
    Family 17, 59
    Sir Edward 42
    Sir James 35
    Sir Richard 30, 35, 36, 41, 42, 50
    Sir Robert 23, 32, 35, 41
Wyatt, James 41, 54
Wydcombe 58

Yaffles, Bonchurch 60
Yarborough, Lord 51
Yaverland Manor 23, 25

79